Dear James

A Woman's Journey Through Grief

Joy LaTorre, M.S., APRN-CNP

ISBN 978-1-63903-309-6 (paperback)
ISBN 978-1-63903-310-2 (digital)

Christian Faith Publishing
832 Park Avenue
Meadville, PA 16335
www.christianfaithpublishing.com

Printed in the United States of America

I would like to first, and most importantly, dedicate this book to my daughter Adriane. Your life gave me the strength I needed to keep fighting through the obstacles we faced as mother and daughter. God knows I did not always do it right. I made a lot of mistakes along the way, but you gave me reason to keep fighting through what seemed impossible. I know in my heart you will one day write the second part to this book. I knew you would the day I brought you back to Boston to board the plane home. I pray I live long enough to read the healing this journey will bring to your own heart. If I am too old to read, promise me you will read me the story.

To my husband, Paul. What would life have looked like for us had it not been graced with your love? Thank you for all you are to me, our children, and grandchildren. I will love you completely until my very last breath. Thank you for picking up the pieces of our shattered hearts.

To God, the Perfect Father, thank you for completing us all.

To every person who will read this book, please understand its purpose was never to shame or bring pain upon anyone.

Its intent was only to share the story with the hearts it may help, encourage, or bring healing to. I have learned when life experiences are shared with a broken world, they possess the potential to bring understanding to what ails the heart. Truth does that. It is not always pleasant, but it does have the power to release us from what keeps us broken. Whatever it may speak to you, receive it. Trust me, it's harder to stay broken.

Introduction

In life, there will always be loss. It is part of our human existence. Many words are used to describe it, but what most accurately defines it? Is separation through death its only definition, the constant daily reminder that we have been affected by it?

It would depend on how you view loss, what situation has caused it, and what scars it has left upon your heart. Loss is complex, clouding hope as it attempts to permeate and overwhelm your soul.

Most have heard the penned words of Alfred Lord Tennyson "'Tis better to have loved and lost than never to have loved at all." Do you agree?[1]

Looking back over personal situations in my own life, if you had asked me the moment it was happening, I would have completely disagreed.

During different times in my life, while completely engulfed in grief, I saw nothing beyond its grasp. There was only darkness.

You may be saying, "Nobody will ever understand my loss!" My answer to you is you are absolutely correct! Loss is an individual experience. It will be your own personal journey, a path only traveled by you. There are other routes journeyed by others, but yours will not be identical. No two paths are the same.

Grief begins at different stages. For some, it begins the moment loss happens. For others, it begins before the loss happens as with anticipatory grief. It can also be delayed when mourning is complicated by other factors. There is no instructional manual. It is an individual process.

Acknowledge it, feel it, and let it take you to a new place on the other side of devastation. If you hear anything I say, please hear this—you can survive!

To every woman and daughter, simply know you are completely loved by the one who created you.

Prologue

The colors were vibrant. Only two words came to mind—sensory explosion. The sidewalk was engorged with life! I found it extremely difficult to navigate through the congestion of people. Gosh, how I dislike crowds! The push. The shove. The feeling of being suffocated in a sea of people. It was difficult; but I kept walking, bumping, squeezing my way through the eternal colors splashed across every inch of my vision.

"This is the city," I grumbled. There was so much noise, movement, color! People without expression hurrying to their destinations. Bright-yellow taxis tightly lined against the sidewalks patiently waiting for their next customers. I could smell the overpopulation of engines, hear traffic with impatient drivers yelling at one another, and an orchestra of out-of-tune horns. In a great effort to elude the pressure closing tighter around me, I found a way to escape it for just a moment. I stopped!

It was amazing how I no longer had to be controlled by all of this endless movement. I took solace in realizing I did not have to be a part of the tumultuous rapids that engulfed me. It was as if I became a cemented object now needing to be avoided by the crowd, a giant rock that had fallen into perfect formation forcing endless waves of people to now flow around me.

I took advantage of my newfound calm. I closed my eyes as I tipped my face toward the sky to get a breath of fresh air. I allowed myself to deposit all my anxiety into its open inviting space. When I opened them, the ocean-blue-painted sky with its soft white clouds captivated me as they tumbled gently through its mixture of vibrant sea blues. I never realized there were so many shades! It was breathtaking.

If only I could remain in this calm, I thought to myself. Savoring every second, as one does the last spoonful of ice cream on a warm summer night, I knew it would not last. I knew better. I was taught by life that moments were only supposed to be moments, not eternity. I drew in one last breath, filling my lungs to capacity, and exhaled all that had invaded me. *Breathe!* I told myself. *You can do this!* Setting my head back on its proper axis, I blew out a breath while simultaneously opening my eyes.

Scanning my surroundings with a new perspective, I began to move. The myriad of colors once again filled my sight. I continued to the corner where I could safely cross the street.

Cautiously stepping off the curb, I continued moving with the morning crowd. At the halfway point, everything around me began to move slower. I was beginning to think I was caught in a time warp as things around me began to change. I was now forced to decelerate my own speed as everything moved slower and slower, until the world around me came to a complete stop.

I was no longer flowing with the crowd but paying close attention to not crash into it. People were like statues, frozen in time. Everything was! It now looked like a still life painting. I saw a briefcase suspended in midair with its gold-plated locks and its four protective standing feet attached on its bottom.

They illuminated intense light as they collided with the sun. The case was hovering behind a man in a dark-royal-blue suit with subtle white lines that would not have been visible to their viewer during natural movement.

Earrings on the ears of a well-dressed woman hung in an unnatural position, along with her long blonde curls suspended in the middle of their bounce. Without movement, colors were more vibrant. They appeared much sharper and fuller.

I continued across the road, being sure to stay within the lines of the crosswalk. *This must be a dream!* I looked at everyone I passed until I met with the adjacent curb from the one I stepped from. Much to my surprise, the moment my right foot touched the curb, everything restarted. My surroundings went from absolute silence to hearing a thousand orchestras playing completely different compositions at the same time. I looked up, and there you were!

You were wearing a long dark coat. You were like a red rose on a black-and-white backdrop. But wait, you were the one without color. Maybe that was why I saw you immediately. Did I only notice you because you were devoid of color, an extreme contrast against the radiant colors that enveloped you? Or was it your long black coat that caught my attention? It was a very warm day. Why were you wearing a coat? You did not move except to occasionally shift your position.

I tried to blend into the colorful crowd so you would not notice me, but you saw me and I knew it. Only then did you move and begin to walk toward me. After you had captured my complete attention, everything around me faded, leaving me completely unaware of my surroundings. The only audible noise was the drumlike sound of my heart. *Am I afraid?* I thought to myself. You continued to approach me. The closer you got to me, the more uncomfortable I became.

I was now suddenly aware I was embarrassed. *What would you think of me? It had been many years since I had seen you. Why did I feel so unattractive?*

I closed my eyes wishing this was not happening. When I opened them, you were so close, if I fully extended my arm, I could have touched you. I could smell you. The Halston cologne you routinely doused yourself in after a hot shower permeated the atmosphere. There was no denying your presence. Your bearded face remained without expression, and you did not attempt to communicate anything to me.

Do I run? I thought to myself but realized I could not. It was not due to inability; it was curiosity that kept me standing there. You looked like a watch thief selling stolen goods on the streets of New York City.

Why did you not say anything? I think never knowing what you were thinking bothered me the most. You refused to talk about anything you attempted to elude. It always added to the rejection I had already been buried under.

I studied you intently, the mood in your eyes, the detail of your movements. You reached with your hand to open the coat. *What is happening?* I thought to myself. *And what exactly does he have inside his coat?*

I watched as you began to open the coat in a slow mechanical motion. I did not feel fear as I had so many other times in your presence. Your expression was much different. Your mood was calm. I

13

knew you well. Because you looked like you were selling something, I was expecting jewelry, I suppose, but the things inside your coat were not shiny. *What were they?*

I was able to see them for just a second. I could only describe them as miniature little trees with soft white buds, but I could not comprehend what they were. There were a lot of them, methodically arranged into perfect little rows. I tried hard to focus, but you were left-handed and your arm was blocking my view. You carefully picked one out of the second row as if selecting the best choice. It was not done in haste. You stepped forward. I looked at you, expecting you to say something, but again you moved in silence. Turning my eyes away from you, I refocused on what you now had in your hand. You placed it onto the left side of my chest, near my heart. Your touch felt so different. It was gentle and meaningful.

After removing your hand, I saw it clearly! Confused, I locked eyes with yours. I could not break the magnetic pull. I wondered what you were thinking. Your eyes seemed to be saying something, but I did not understand their language. You smiled gently. The corners of your mouth turned toward the fine lines at the edges of your eyes. *What does this mean?* I thought to myself. My eyes filled with tears as I attempted to speak. There was not enough time.

After closing your coat, you quickly turned and walked away. Although I did not see her standing there, she was watching us. She took hold of my hand and together we watched you disappear. Your colorless appearance was somehow repainted by the colors around you, allowing you to fade into the vibrant crowd. Once again you were gone.

I bolted upright, wiped the sweat from my face, and rubbed my eyes. *Where am I? What day is it? Calm down. It is Saturday. No work. It is still dark. Breathe. It was just a dream. But what exactly did it mean?* I allowed my head to crash down onto the pillow. The soft down feathers somehow cradled my mind and lulled me back to sleep. I did not know how much longer I slept before I was once again snatched from the quiet.

"Why is this phone ringing?" I grumbled. The sunlight pierced through the window setting the room ablaze. Covering my head with the blanket, I attempted to drown out the sound that penetrated my once-silent room. My husband had gone out for an early morning hunt. He kissed me before he left the house, so I knew it was not him. The phone continued to ring.

I managed to get one eye open in an attempt to see who it was. I did not recognize the number. What could be important enough to wake me up so early on a Saturday morning? After greeting the person on the other end of the phone, I realized it was my youngest sister. I immediately knew something was wrong.

"I'm sorry I called so early," she said. "But I felt that I needed to tell you. It's only right that you know."

"Lil?" I answered. "Are you okay? Don't be sorry. It's okay," I assured her.

"I didn't know if I should tell you," she continued. "But I felt that someone should let you know." I could hear the brokenness in the tone of her voice, the hesitation.

"Know what?" I asked, my heart now picking up its pace.

"James," she said. There was a long pause before she continued. "I am so sorry," she said again. I could now feel anxiety working its way through my flesh. I held my breath.

"James died yesterday. I thought it was only right that someone told you," she repeated. I sat there motionless, trying to understand what exactly she just told me. A moment of confusion, perhaps. Maybe shock? I was not quite sure.

"James," I uttered back. "He died?" I immediately felt numb. It is a feeling so many have described when confronted with the finality of death.

The *I-have-to-find-my-way-out-of-this-nightmare phenomenon.*

"Are you sure he died?" I asked in disbelief.

"Yes," she said softly.

"Thank you for calling," I said. *I felt like I had just swallowed my heart.* Panic had begun to over-whelm me.

"Adriane," I said. *My daughter was now my only concern.*

"Are you okay? I didn't mean to upset you," she said, now crying.

"I'm okay. Thank you, Lil. I have to call Adriane. I love you," I told her before hitting the red discon-nect button on my cell phone.

.

February 20, 2016
Saturday
8:10 a.m.

I sat on my bed for a moment, remembering the evening before. My husband and I had gone to dinner with some friends. On our way back to the car, as our husbands walked ahead of us, my friend Donna and I were talking about one of Adele's newest songs, "Hello."[2]

As we walked across the cold parking lot, I belted out the words to teach her the song. I had listened to it many times while driving alone in my car. In my heart, I knew exactly who I attached the song to, but I did not share this information with her. "I must have called a thousand times to tell you I'm sorry for everything that I've done," I sang, leaving the parking lot much quieter as we climbed into the back seat closing the doors.

It is over now, I thought as I sat on my bed. *I will never get to hear the words I had attached to James. Words I had so desperately needed to hear him say. Words he would never speak. Death had silenced him forever.*

July 8, 2016
Friday
6:15 p.m.

I opened the garage door without a plan in mind. I knew I had to go for a ride. I knew this day would come when I first brought him into my home. The process leading to this night was difficult. His death left so many unanswered questions lingering. Lost opportunities. Time, I thought we would have, to someday talk about all that had happened between us.

I had worked through it, or so I thought.

Intense rage periodically surfaced over the last five months but not to this extent. I had to deal with it tonight, and I knew it. I felt discontent throughout most of the day. I was irritated and short-tempered. My husband knew there was something bothering me, but to be honest, I did not know what it was when he asked me. I only knew I was angry. After pulling into our driveway, I entered the house finding myself heading toward the hutch located in the dining room. I knew exactly what I was going in there to get but had no idea what I was going to do with it. I did not remove my jacket. I knew I was not staying.

I opened the hutch, toppling over some of the crystal glasses as I reached in to get the little black jar. One of the glasses fell on top of the tiara Adriane had worn on her wedding day. It was delicately placed in her silky dark hair. It sparkled like fine chiseled diamonds. It now sat inside the hutch on top of her bridal long opera gloves. The gloves were made of delicate white silk. I remember the day she wore them both. It was magical. She was radiant. Her slender petite fingers fit them so perfectly. A fairy-tale princess. I will always remember how she looked up at her husband. She gazed at him with such love and trust. It was a look I had never seen in her eyes.

As my hand contacted the little black jar, my past and present collided, creating the perfect storm. The "anger" stage of grief had been unleashed and there was no way to rein it back in. I knew it instantly.

July 8, 2016
Friday
6:35 p.m.

Dear James,

Months ago, I emptied you into a bowl to see what you looked like. It was odd seeing you all white. Your favorite color was black. I do not know what I was expecting to see. When I unscrewed the ornate

JOY LATORRE, M.S., APRN-CNP

ceramic lid, I could not believe how so much dust, fit into such a small urn.

I hesitated at first. It took about a half hour before I mustered up the guts to even open the jar. All kinds of thoughts entered my mind. If I opened it, would I unleash your spirit into my home? Would you always be there trying to find your way back to the rest of you? I guess it reminded me of a television show I watched as a kid. Did you watch it too? "I Dream of Jeannie." Do you remember that show James? I always wondered how she squeezed herself into that lamp and here you were, just like her, compacted!

I am sorry, I needed to see you. I had to know what you looked like. Were you crushed bone or were you finely ground like baby powder? Curiosity got the best of me and I went to the kitchen to get a bowl. I placed a piece of newspaper on top of my table and slowly emptied you into the bowl. I managed to get all of you into it safely without dropping you onto the floor or table. Staring at the contents of what was supposed to be you, I wondered which parts of all these tiny particles could possibly be. Crazy thought I know.

I hovered my finger over the contents of the bowl for a while. Why did I wait so long? Did I think it would burn if I touched you?

I had shaken an urn once to hear what it sounded like but never opened one, never mind touching the contents inside. I decided to stop thinking James. I closed my eyes, held my breath, and plunged my finger into you. The moment we contacted, I gasped and drew in air as if I had just surfaced from being underneath water, desperately needing oxygen. I cannot explain what I felt. You did not feel soft like powder. You had a gritty texture. I opened my eyes as I began to circle my finger around the contents of the bowl; at times rubbing the substance of you between my thumb and index finger.

They say grief takes on all forms of behavior and I was okay that this was one of them. As I continued to stir you, I wondered if any of these particles could be the finger you had me permanently ink my initials into so many years ago. Do you remember that James? We all skipped school and hung out in a vacant garage on the side of an abandoned house. There had to be about ten of us. Some days everyone drank Boon's Farm wine and played spin the bottle. I did not drink it. The effect it had on people was not something I was fond of. I remember that day because it was the first time you kissed me.

On this day, we were engaged in a different activity. We were wrapping white thread around sewing needles, dipping them in murky black India Ink. I don't know why it was called that? Is that where it came from? A thick small glass jar with a rubber stopper held the ink. After holding an ice cube on your finger until you could not feel it any longer, I remember the first thing you had me make as I poked your skin with the needle innumerous times. It was a cross. You had asked me to be your girlfriend the day before. I said yes, and today you wanted me to embed my initials into your skin, one on each side of the cross.

As the memory faded, returning me back to a more conscious state, I realized I was still stirring the contents of the bowl. James, I wondered, if any part of this was your heart, I so desperately tried to be enough for? I continued to stir you as so many questions invaded my mind.

I did understand I would have to destroy the bowl. I knew it was no longer eligible for consuming food, but how was I going to get you back into the jar I poured you out of? It took a little bit of thought, but I did manage to get you back in there. I rolled up a piece of paper and made a little funnel. I learned that from you. Do you remember that? We were riding around in your car and ran out of gas. It was a metallic blue SS Monte Carlo. You chose a cherry scented car freshener to hang from the rear-view mirror. I still think of you every time I smell the scent. We walked to a gas station holding hands. I stood watching you as you pumped gasoline into a gallon sized plastic milk jug you took out of the trunk of the car. You must have kept it there for such an occasion. We had no idea how we were going to get it into the gas tank and decided to roll up the cover from a school notebook you had on the back seat beside a history book. Amazingly, it worked.

I did learn some cool things from you. If it worked for gasoline, it would undoubtedly work for this. I rolled the paper the same way you did that day. It was a perfect way to get you back in there. I was careful with you. I was petrified I would leave parts of you out. I did not know many things at that moment, but I did realize one. Our journey was beginning. Grief had begun. Many would have thought it started the day I saw your lifeless body months before, but it did not. It began when I touched you.

James, you are not going to believe this but the first thought that came to my mind was to taste the powder you now were. Gross right? I could not help it. It instantly reminded me of confectionary sugar. I can only be honest I suppose. Grief is never right or wrong James, it is simply grief. It looks different for every individual. My thoughts were a bit twisted I suppose.

Do not worry James. I did not do it! It was just a thought, as I stared at you clinging to the tip of the index finger I used to stir you. I was however relieved the thought quickly passed. How would I ever explain that to anyone? If I had put my finger into my mouth James, would it have been defined as cannibalism, although you no longer had any flesh?

27

I had heard of people taking cremated ashes, mixing them into tattoo ink, and having it injected into their skin so their loved one would always be with them. What is that considered? If I did that, you would then be a permanent part of my own body through deliberate infusion. This disturbed me more than the thought of tasting you. Thankfully, this thought was also fleeting. I could not inject you into my skin James. You were always trying to escape me. What if you found a way to rip your way out?

Okay enough of that. I screwed the little lid back onto the jar and placed you back between the crystal glasses. I must admit, you matched my décor quite nicely.

July 8, 2016
Friday
7:01 p.m.

When I placed the little black urn into the hutch back in February, I knew the day would arrive when I would have to come to terms with all the pain I had stuffed throughout the years. Here it was. Our final journey together was about to begin.

I put the little urn into the black leather case attached to the windshield of my motorcycle. James would be secure from the wind. It was a warm evening for a ride, and so off we went.

I had no idea where I was going but found myself heading toward the place where I had first set eyes on him. I tucked a pen and a hardcover journal into the compartment beside the little jar. *Funny*, I thought to myself. *I did not know what I was going to do twenty-eight years ago when our relationship ended. However, this time I completely understood I would end up where I was supposed to be. This time, I trusted the journey.*

February 20, 2016
Saturday
9:31 a.m., United States
3:31 p.m., Zaandam, Netherlands

"Hi, honey. It's Mom."

"Hi, Mom!" she said in her jovial little voice.

She was not so little anymore. She was thirty-one years old, a mother of two beautiful girls, and a wife of nine years living more than 3,500 miles on the other side of the Atlantic Ocean. I never wanted Adriane to live with any regret in life as I had. She knew me well. She immediately knew there was something wrong. She was good at understanding my tones.

I had paced around the house for a while before making the final decision to call her. Anger and disbelief, mixed with nausea, played toss with me for a little while before I decided to dial her number. I knew I needed to tell her.

"What's wrong, Mom?" she asked.

I hesitated before answering. "There is no other way to tell you this, Adriane, but James died yesterday."

"He died? How did he die?" she asked.

"I don't have all the answers right now. I only found out this morning. You do not have to come, but if you want to, Daddy and I will get you a ticket to bring you home. You only get one chance, Adriane. I had to make a similar decision once myself, and I often wonder if I made the wrong one. My own biological father was shot and killed when I was twenty years old. I had the chance to see him before he died. I did not go. I did not have a relationship with him either, but I often wished I went. This is your choice, Adriane. We will support the decision you make, but you do not have a lot of time to decide."

She needed some time to talk with her husband and said she would call me back. Eventually, she decided to come, but it would take a miracle to get her here. The day had just started on my side of the earth, but on hers, it was nearing evening.

We worked hard, and twenty-four hours from our initial call, we got her as close to Rhode Island as we could. We had to take a six-hour drive to Pennsylvania to pick her up at the Philadelphia International Airport. She had just enough time to come home, buy something to wear, and try getting some sleep. We had a wake to attend the following evening.

The six-hour time difference made the adjustment more difficult. His death only complicated her sleeping pattern. I suppose death never has an appropriate time. We don't decide. It does.

February 22, 2016
Monday
4:30 p.m.

I remember getting dressed to go to the service. It had been many years since anyone in his family had seen me. I wondered if they would even recognize me. Would they recognize Adriane? I went into the bedroom where she was getting ready, to get a brush. I could tell she was nervous. She was quiet. I was trying to deal with my emotions, but I was also worried about hers.

My husband told me if I needed to attend the wake alone with Adriane, he would completely understand. That was not even a thought in my mind. He was my husband, and I wanted him there. Adriane wanted him beside her also. We finished dressing, grabbed the keys, and headed for the door.

When inside the car, I turned toward her in the back seat. "Are you sure you want to do this?" I asked one last time. "I need to do this, Mom," she responded. As her mother, I completely understood.

July 8, 2016
Friday
7:32 p.m.

Dear James,

We arrived at our first stop. I shut off the engine of my motorcycle, took out the journal and pen, and decided to write to you. I am on the road we all called "The Boulevard" adjacent to your sister's house. I honestly do not know if she still lives there. Your parents owned it. You had told me when we were dating, it used to be a convenience store before it was made into a duplex. It resembles the shape of a corner store. Nothing has changed here. It looks the same. It was on this road that I met you. You were such a quiet boy. That is what attracted me to you. There was a time I thought I would have you forever. What was I thinking? Such a naïve, young girl. There is so much history between us on this road. It is the place it began. Do you remember that night we first saw each other? I can still remember the exact spot.

I am looking at my surroundings, and so many memories are flashing before me. I am so angry. What do I do James? What am I even doing here? I cannot believe after twenty-eight years, I still feel so rejected by you. I knew what I had to do the moment I asked the question and unscrewed the top of the tiny black and gold ceramic urn. I was not afraid this time. I had already seen you in this state. I had already touched you. Without hesitation, I poured some of what had once been you into the palm of my hand. The street was eerily quiet, not at all what I remembered. The air was warm. There was a small gentle breeze that seemed to softly caress my face. I looked around and wondered how many people were watching me. I am sure nobody was. It was just the anxiety of being back here.

I am parked on the side of the road on a Harley Davidson writing in a book. I am filled with anxiety. Would anyone even recognize me? I concluded that it was highly unlikely. It had been twenty-eight years since I had been here.

As I held the tiny particles that were a portion of you, a multitude of thoughts flooded my mind. Most of the thoughts caused me to feel intense anger. It gave me the confidence I needed to open my hand and release you. I watched you, the white chalk-like substance as it fell to the ground finding its way to the side of my front tire, as I released you. A cold chill rushed through me and I shuttered.

Oh James, there you are. You settled on the ground right where you stood, the day I first saw you. I may have sat there staring at the ground if my thoughts had not been interrupted. Ironically, from the house directly in front of me, flowing from an open window, was the song by Adele I had belted out in a parking lot five months prior.

I must admit James, the timing is a bit strange. I often read about this phenomenon many call "signs" after experiencing loss. The music startled me. It gave me the unsettling feeling that you were trying to reach me somehow. I am sorry if you were. I had to dismiss you. I am just not ready to listen to anything you are trying to say. The pain is too heavy. Do you know what I learned about unresolved grief? When the person who had once left you dies, it is often perceived to be their last act of abandonment. James, it is overwhelming. I will never get the chance to know if you ever felt regret for walking away from us. Did you ever wonder how we were, where had we ended up, or even what we looked like?

I shut my eyes tightly, adamantly refusing to let any of this pain escape and roll down my face.

I refuse to cry James. I cried many tears during our time together and I will not let myself be the broken, desperate-to-be-loved person I once was. I am in control now and you will do what I say. You will go wherever I take you.

Guess what James? You cannot leave this time! I understand I do not have all of you, but then again, I guess I never did.

However, this part of you is mine and no one can take you from me. I am going to do whatever I want with you and no one can stop me. Honestly, James I feel a sense of empowerment. So many people interfered. Too many people had an opinion. Not this time! The choice is mine.

Look at you! You look pathetic stuck to my hand. I remember looking that way once too, the pathetic young girl so eager to be loved. Don't worry, you will get over it, James. I had to. I did not have a choice then and you do not have one now. Tell me James, do you feel vulnerable? Do you feel unwanted? Tell me, how does this make you feel? Do you think it felt the way I did?

I wiped my left hand onto my jeans, put my helmet back on, and wrote a few more words in the journal before closing it.

Let's go around the block to Irving Road shall we James?

The house where James grew up was located on Irving Road. It was a house I went to many times. It was here that he asked me to be his girlfriend on October 16, 1982. There were good memories, and at some, I giggled. But I was on a mission, and honoring him was not one of them.

Here, in front of this house, one memory took hostage of all the others. I looked at the white powder on the front of my jeans with disgust. I parked the bike across the street from the house and took out the journal.

July 8, 2016
Friday
8:02 p.m.

Dear James,

Look at my jeans, they are filthy. Why couldn't you have loved me? This memory is too painful, but I know I must watch it play out before me. I am not alone in this rejection, and I was not that day. Thankfully, she did not yet possess the ability to understand. I am trying to calm myself by rubbing more of you onto my jeans, but it is not working.

I remember a time I came here to see you. I was pregnant and came to your house to bring you something. Honestly, I cannot remember what it was, but I do remember why I did it. We had been split up for some foolish reason I am sure. I was about four months pregnant. Your father answered and told me you did not want to see me. I insisted. He left the door open and disappeared into the house. I did not follow him because I was not invited in. I wanted you to come to the door so badly James. I wanted you to see how much our baby was growing. I needed you to love me; to love our baby.

Your father returned and told me you did not want to talk. You would not even come to the door! I did not have any words. Neither did your father. He slowly closed the door. I took that as my que to leave. I turned before I heard the door meet its frame. I was so devastated. You were not even curious.

You left me standing there feeling unwanted and alone. How can a memory possess the ability to force me to feel it twice? James it honestly feels more intense than it did all those years ago.

I know this is another place I
must leave you. I wish I could take
you right to the door, but the property has a new owner, and I know
they would not approve of my plan.
I will get as close as I can. Hold on
James, I will be right back.

I placed the journal onto the seat of the bike
and walked across the street, feeling somewhat nau-
seous. I could only get as close as the front of the
house. I was scared. The house was set back from the
street. There was grass on a lower level near the road
and a set of stone stairs that led up to the house. I
could not bring myself to walk up the stairs to the
door where I stood thirty-two years ago. My heart
began to pound. I quickly returned to the safety
of my bike. I picked up the journal and continued
where I had left off.

Dear James,

That was harder than I thought. I
know I was young, but I had been
abandoned by so much in my
life already. I remember believing
things would be different now that
we were starting our own family. It

would be different than the one I grew up in.

We never talked about my childhood James, but I remember being a small child in state custody wanting so badly for someone to want me, and there I was, a young adult feeling the same cold rejection. It was too much for me to handle. I felt you mixing with the sweat that was in the palm of my hand as I stood in front of the house. I bent down and pretended to tie my boot and wiped you onto the grass. It was the only way I could put you there in the center of the memory. I walked back across the street and got back onto my bike.

I could feel the stinging of tears that so desperately wanted me to open the flood gate and release them. I could not yet find the lever to open it. Where do we go now James? Again, before pulling my helmet back on, I wiped you onto my jeans.

I realized my mood was beginning to slightly change. I did not quite know how, but I began to feel different than when I had started this journey. I felt more controlled, not so entangled in pain. I left my house with such rage, such a feeling of wanting James to pay somehow, making up for everything that was now surfacing, everything I had kept buried for so long.

I began to understand what I was doing and what I needed to do. I started the bike and began to ride, leaving that particular memory on Irving Road. Feeling somehow lighter, I rounded the corner, taking a right turn onto Warwick Avenue. I passed the house where I lived when I was in high school.

Anxiety swept over me. It was the building directly after the house that caught my attention. I turned into its parking lot. I parked my bike in a spot which allowed me full view of the entrance. I reached into the black pouch and I took out the journal.

July 8, 2016
Friday
8:12 p.m.

Dear James,

I am now at Eddy's 529. It is the local neighborhood pub. Do you remember this place? I was always looking for you. Always trying to get you to come home. Always silently begging you to want to be with me. You were not even old enough to be in a bar, how did you even get in there? I wondered now but did not think of it then.

I must say, the place has not changed much. I felt a sense of calm, knowing I would not be caught looking for you this time. A man is crossing the parking lot looking at me. I guess it must be impressive to see a woman on a Harley. I remember the one you had. You got it after our relationship ended. I never got to ride on it but hey, we made up for lost time. I gave you a ride on mine. You would have been impressed! It is a 2016 Harley Davidson Dyna Street Bob with a 103 cubic inch Twin Cam-Six Speed, 650-pound bike! You should feel special James. I have only had it for about three months. You are my very first passenger.

The past pulled me quickly back. Every time I went looking for you, I could not find you. I wanted to find you. Trust me James, it was not by lack of effort. Why did I ever believe I could have made you come home with me and Adriane? I once again reached for you in the little ceramic urn. I opened the cover. Paying closer attention this time, I noticed there were different sized pieces of you as I dumped more of you into my hand. Some pieces appeared clumpy. Maybe pieces had settled on the bottom like flour does when it is exposed to moisture. The warm outside air was not what you had been used to during the last five months. You were protected from the outside elements at my house.

At that moment, I decided to separate you. It took a little while, but I did not have any other plans. I put the powdered portion of you back into the urn. I stuffed the small solid pieces into the left pocket of my jeans, which now resembled a finger painting created by a few toddlers who all used the same white paint.

I kept a piece in my hand about the size of the diamond you had bought me when you told me you wanted to be with me forever. Remember that promise ring? It was supposed to signify the promise you made to one day make me your wife.

Promise rings. That is what they called them all those years ago. The ring was only a small chip of a diamond, but to me it was the tangible proof you would always love me. It was a promise you never kept. Sadly, promises were a thing you we not good at keeping. I took one last look at the door on the side of the building.

James, I wonder if subconsciously I am still waiting to see if you will open the door and step into the parking lot. Understanding it is impossible, I took the small piece of you and dropped it in the parking lot just in case I ever decided I wanted to come back and see if I could find you here.

February 22, 2016
Monday
5:18 p.m.

We arrived at the funeral home. Adriane looked so grown up. I was so proud of her. She was a considerate young woman. I could feel her emotions as they collided with my own. I believe a mother can deal with her own pain, but when it comes to her child, she becomes enraged. A part of me did not want her to even care, but I knew that was an impossibility. I wanted this because it was so easy for him to walk away and never look back. I guess I believed if she chose not to care, she could escape the feelings of abandonment. As we walked toward the building, I was momentarily locked in my thoughts.

I wondered if James understood every little girl learns about relationships through the love of her father. Did Adriane feel what I felt? I knew my own pain. I knew my own disappointment when it came to a father that walked away from me. I think that is what made this so much harder. I so desperately wanted James to love her. I understood that Adriane and I shared similar pain.

However, in this situation, it was my own rejection by James, as well as his abandonment of our daughter, that overwhelmed me.

There is always that part of a child, even as they become an adult, that is still haunted by questions. Why did he leave? Was it my fault? Why did he not come back? Why was I not enough?

As young girls continue to mature into adolescence, they are haunted by another reality. When they are denied the love of a biological father and are not blessed with a man to father them, they do not understand what love is supposed to look like. A father displays this to her by the love he shows her mother. It gives her the understanding of what love is supposed to look like when she first falls in love.

Sadly, at times, the blueprints are left blank.

Looking back over my own childhood and having been placed in the custody of the state of Rhode Island, I understood why my mother could not take care of us at the time, but I always wondered why my father did not keep us with him. My mother could not take care of her children while consuming the amount of alcohol she did daily, but where was my father? I thought daddies loved their daughters.

They say a father is a little girl's first crush, her first knight in shining armor. He is the man who protects her from the things that frighten her and the things that go bump in the night. There was a lot of bumping going on that I did not know how to navigate through.

My blueprints were blank. I did not understand this was not what healthy relationships looked like.

The only blueprints I had were the ones my mother displayed. I believed that being physically struck by a man was because he loved you. Why would I not think that? My mother and her husband got along after he beat her up the night before. Her husband told her how much he loved her, and this is what his love for her made him do. She seemed to agree. However, I was beginning to understand the blueprints I was shown were drafted the wrong way, and sadly, I did not know how to alter them.

Looking back now, it was most likely the reason I attached myself prematurely to any man that promised to love me. My emotional needs were screaming for someone to hear me, and I really believed James was listening. Sadly, my relationship began to replicate the life of my mother.

February 22, 2016
Monday
5:30 p.m.

During the drive to the wake, we were all quiet. We arrived at the funeral and parked the car. As we approached the door, we were welcomed by a tall man who obviously worked for the funeral home. I held Adriane's hand as we entered. It was elegantly decorated. I could feel the softness of the rug under my feet. The scent of lilies enveloped me. I always loved their fragrance. We headed down the hall as directed. I was grateful there was not a line.

I felt the sting of reality as I read his name on the little black sign in miniature white letters with an arrow directing us to the room on the left. The moment we walked into the room, I heard the song "Simple Man" playing by Lynyrd Skynyrd as pictures flashed across a screen that had been set up in the corner on the left side of the room.

We entered the room and quietly took a seat. My daughter was not ready to go up to the front and see James, and I was not going to cause her additional stress. She was going to decide when and how she wanted to do this. I, on the other hand, wanted to go immediately. I wanted to see what he looked like after all these years. Did he look the same as the memory in my head? Did he still have a beard and that annoying little cowlick that made his hair stick up on the right side of his head? How he disliked it.

His casket was surrounded by his children and their mother. Adriane told me she felt like an intruder. I wanted so desperately for her to not feel left out, but she did. I wanted her to make her appearance known, but she waited. Waiting was something she used to do as a little girl. Maybe it was a learned behavior. She waited for a father who never showed.

July 8, 2016
Friday
8:37 p.m.

As I pulled out from Eddie's 529, I began to travel south down Warwick Avenue. I did not get too far. I saw a building and once again was overtaken by a memory that greatly disturbed me. I pulled in, shut off my bike, put down the kick stand, and reached for the journal.

This place is more difficult to look at. It was not only me whom James rejected here. Here, he made his decision about Adriane. She was approximately two years old, and he was supposed to pick her up and take her for the day. She waited. She cried. He did not come.

Angered by her disappointment once again, I carried her to where I thought he was. I was right. My guess was accurate. It was not early. He was supposed to pick Adriane up at eleven o'clock, and it was now one o'clock.

My friend had seen me walking on my way there and picked me up. When I saw his car, we pulled into the driveway. He was at his brother's house. I left Adriane in the car with my friend and walked up the stairs to knock on the door. The stairs went up to the door at the back part of the house. I knocked until someone decided to open it. The moment I saw him,

I knew it must have been a long night. It made sense.
He was still sleeping. I asked him why he never came
to get Adriane, and he told me he went to a concert
the night before.

We had an argument about his lack of respon-
sibility, and I ended up at the bottom of the stairs,
not by my own effort. James told me that day it was
better if I took Adriane and went my own way in life
and he would go his.

He was dating a new girl. She was now standing
behind him. I knew who she was. She lived in the
neighborhood. She was younger than us by a couple
of years. She was pretty; there was no denying that.

He had told me once I was boring because I
did not like to party. I wondered if she possessed
the quality he told me I lacked. After all, when I
knocked on the door, she was sleeping too.

After turning off the engine of my bike, I took
out my journal and began to write.

Dear James,

I am looking at the stairs from
where my bike is. There is no light-
ing in the area where the stairs are
located, making it appear later
than it is. It looks so lonely back
there in the dark. I wish I did not

have to do this, but you left me no choice. I know I must leave you at the bottom of these stairs the same way you left me.

Your new girlfriend knew what you did. She was standing behind you when you pushed me. You did many things to me that I could cover up James, but not this time. I was humiliated. You made your feelings about me quite clear. The last thing I heard before getting up to return to my friend's car was the slamming of your brother's apartment door. Tell me James, did you go back to bed?

I feel sadness. I cannot determine if it is the past memory forcing its way back into the present, or if I feel bad that I must leave you in the dark by yourself. I would never want anyone to feel the way I did that day. To be honest, I am hesitant. Why did it have to end up this way? I have pain in my heart, but I understand this somehow needs to be covered, and the only one that can make it right is you. I gathered

up a small pile of you and placed
you gently on the bottom step. I
turned away and started walking.
I am sorry I must leave you here
James. I hope you understand. I
was gentle and respectful. I did not
push you.

Once again, the tears welled up in my eyes. They
still did not spill over, but this time, they did reach
the brim of my eyelids. I was finding it harder to
restrain them. I took a deep breath as I began walking back to my motorcycle. I felt this was a cruel
thing to do. *How sad to leave him alone*, I thought.
I turned to face the stairs for a moment and understood why. It was dark and lonely. *No one should ever
be left alone like that*, I thought as I pulled my bike
back onto the main road.

July 8, 2016
Friday
9:15 p.m.

I pulled into the parking lot of the funeral
home. Tonight, the lot was empty. I parked my bike
off to the side of the building, deciding to spend
some time writing what I was thinking as we rode
together on this beautiful summer night.

Dear James,

There was a time when I did not know what I was going to do with you. I did ask my husband permission before I brought you into our home. I set you in the hutch. Occasionally, I would glance at you, wishing I was given the opportunity to say goodbye, knowing that you had said your goodbye many years ago. Now, as hard as it was, I knew I had to navigate through and figure out how I was going to accept it.

James, I learned that one does not choose when grief decides to fall out of the closest, we try to stuff it into. You can attempt to hide from it, but it finds you anyway. It slowly builds until it explodes. It causes you to do things you normally would not do. It is true James, I never thought I would find myself screaming at a little black and gold urn with my finger pointed at it.

I was having a stressful day and happened to pass the hutch where I had set you. You became the target of my anger and I lost it! I went up to you and let you have it! Grief fell out of the closet. It found me.

"Look at you!" I screamed at the top of my lungs. Look what you did to yourself. You thought life was going to be better without us! Tell me James, please tell me, was it? Did you find the excitement you were so desperately searching for? I do not want to hear your excuses, so save it!

Yeah, yeah, yeah. I know you were young. That was always the excuse! Well guess what? Here is some reality for you! So was I! That is not an excuse to leave your child! You know what I think? I think you were an idiot. All the lies. All of the cheating. You should have stayed where you belonged. Well guess what? Now you have to!! You are staying right there! You-will-move-when-I-say-you-can! This time you cannot hide from me, and people cannot lie for you. I know where you are now, and you-are-not-moving! I will decide when you can.

And until I am ready, sit there and think hard about what you lost!

Oh James. If anyone could have seen into my home, they would have thought I was insane. I had so much to say that could never be said. Maybe this was my way of saying it.

Death denied me the opportunity. Tears are falling. They are stinging my face.

In an instant, the memory faded, reminding me I was sitting on my bike at the funeral home. It was getting late, and I realized I had to finish what I came here to do. The first thing I noticed were the cameras on the front of the building. *How am I going to pull this off?* I thought. I decided to continue writing, allowing myself more time to decide how I was going to execute this. Before I had the chance to think out a plan, I was pulled back into February when I last saw you here, the last day Adriane was in your presence.

Dear James,

Adriane was ready. She took my hand and did not say a word. Both our hands were perspiring, morphing into one. She understood me and I understood her.

"Are you sure you are ready?" I asked. With tear filled eyes, she nodded. My husband felt he should not go but Adriane insisted. He gently urged us ahead of himself as he quietly moved into the aisle walking closely behind. As we got closer to the casket, your children were hovering over you crying. I felt her hesitate, and I felt sad for your children. None of this was their fault. I turned my attention back to Adriane.

"Are you okay?" I whispered to her. Her response overwhelmed me. Earlier that day she asked my other two children to accompany her. My son thought she should not even attend your wake, and my daughter did not want to go. She said she would be uncomfortable. Honestly, neither of them would have been more uncomfortable than Adriane was at that very moment.

"I feel alone" she said. "They all have each other. I do not belong here."

We bypassed your casket as she did not want to intrude on your children. We walked directly over to your family to offer our condolences. They remembered her, which may have helped a small amount even though one of your brothers called her Andrea. I quickly corrected him trying to shield Adriane from any more feelings of rejection. I wanted to believe it was nerves, but I knew the latter was the truth. He did not remember her name. I was not angry at him. It was not his job to remember she existed. It was yours. You were the one who walked out of her life by the age of three.

James, could you see her from wherever you are? I was so proud of her. A beautiful young woman without animosity.

On the way back to our seats, she gave her condolences to your children without approaching your casket. What an absolute cumbersome situation and she was beautifully graceful.

We reclaimed our seats near the back of the room. She sat quietly. Toward the end of the service, when the room began to clear, we decided to pay our respects at your casket. My heart started to pound. I fixed my eyes on the decorative wood of your casket trying not to look at you. I was not ready. The first thing I looked at was not your face. It was your hands. Your left hand was lying on top of your right. Your entire hand was covered with a black and gray shaded tattoo. You wore no wedding band, although you were married. I reached down and touched my own, twisting it around my finger, thankful for the man I married. I must admit, I wanted to lift your left hand to see if my initials were still there. That would have been odd. I did not know if they were stuck together with adhesive to prevent unwanted movement, but I did wonder. Your left hand was covered with a tattoo, the artwork was impeccable.

I finally turned my eyes toward your face. Your eyes were the same almond shape. Your eyelashes were long. I had remembered watching you sleep many times when we were together. Your eyes were so beautiful. Your hair was almost fully gray. Your beard had one area that still contained dark hair. The contrast was odd. It made it look like a bald spot. You looked so much older than forty-nine. If you had escaped death, just two days later, you would have made it to fifty.

Although I had not seen you in many years, when I saw people who knew our history together, they did not hesitate to tell me about your life.

Remembering some of what I was told, and looking at you now, I felt sad. As angry as I was at you, I never spoke badly about you to Adriane.

After listening to my mother's husband tell me how pathetic my

own father was, I completely understood if you tell a child their other
parent is bad, you are subconsciously
telling the child half of them is bad.
She was half of you, and she is not
bad.

I wanted to know if you really
had Adriane's name tattooed on
your chest as your sister had told me
many years ago. She said you put
it there after the birth of another
daughter, but she was not ours. You
claimed two, yet walked away from
one, mine. Was it guilt that made
you put it there? I wanted just a
small amount of time alone with
you so I could investigate. I never
got the chance.

If I had thought of it at the
time, I would have waited until your
family left and reentered the building to ask if Adriane and I could
have some time alone with you. I
am sure the funeral home workers
would not have objected if I looked,
everyone else was touching you. I
often wonder if I had been given the

opportunity, would I have been able to do it?

James, Adriane has pain but not their pain. She has emotional pain caused by your abandonment. Your family had the pain of your physical loss. I wonder James, which do you think is worse?

We left the funeral and returned home. Adriane had become somewhat silent. We gave her space. My husband, the man who loved and fathered her, was so gentle with her. I did not know how he even felt.

I do know he was worried about Adriane. She had so much to process. She went downstairs to spend some time alone. She was not scheduled to return home for another few days. My husband and I had tea and talked about how I was feeling. He is an admirable man.

He did not stand in front of the casket. He said it was not his place. He did, however, stand directly behind me and Adriane, displaying respect to James and love and protection of us.

Before we entered the building that night, he prayed with us both. I thought to myself, *I have James to thank for him. My husband is the best gift James ever gave Adriane by walking away.*

We spent the next couple of days spending time with each other and family. We kept things light. She was glad to be home for a little while.

February 26, 2016
Thursday
9:30 p.m.

Adriane spent most of the early evening packing up to get ready for her flight home. I was sitting on the couch watching *American Idol*. Kelly Clarkson returned to the show to be a guest judge for the live top ten show. Adriane came upstairs when she was done packing. She was in her pajamas. She took a blanket and sat on the couch beside me. We both became quiet when it was time for her to return home. Her leaving has always been hard for me. I did not speak. I knew she had a lot on her mind. She would talk when she was ready.

There, before our eyes, was a very pregnant Kelly Clarkson singing a new rendition of her song, "Piece by Piece."[3] She sang it in a different tempo than its original version. However, it had been the first time either of us had heard it. I watched my daughter's face as this emotional performance was clearly sung about the rejection and absence of Kelly's own father in front of millions of television viewers. I immediately knew my daughter related.

Piece by piece he collected me
up off the ground where you abandoned things
Piece by piece he filled the holes
that you burned in me at six years
old.
He never walked away, He never
asked for money.
He takes care of me He loves me.

The last line Adriane heard her sing opened an ocean of tears she had barricaded over the last few days.

Piece by piece he restored my faith
that a man can be kind and a father
could stay.

The very next thing I heard was the sound of Adriane sobbing. After holding her for a while, she let me know exactly how she was feeling.

"Mom," she said, "I understand you have been hurt by him, but boyfriends and girlfriends break up all the time. People get divorced. I was his blood, Mom. I was not his girlfriend. I was his first child. Why did he leave me?" I remained quiet because I did not have the answers she both desperately wanted and deserved.

She dedicated Clarkson's song that night on her Facebook page to her husband who loved her exactly as she was created, and my husband, her father, the man who loved her completely as she was the moment he became her daddy at the age of four—a visually impaired little girl whose biological father walked away, a father who did not stay.

Adriane Pasterkamp-LaTorre
February 26, 2016 · Cranston, RI, United States · 👥 ▾

Thank you Paul LaTorre and Sebastiaan Pasterkamp for picking up my pieces. #powerful #kellyclarkson

July 8, 2016
Friday
11:08 p.m.

Dear James,

I cannot believe I just did that. I rode out of the parking lot of the funeral home. It was the very last place I had seen you. I honestly thought it was the end of our journey, but after heading back to my home, my attention was drawn to another place, a small bridge. We will get to why I am here but let me tell you what happened in the parking lot.

I had to find a way to leave a piece of you there without the cameras recording what I was about to do. It could not be the powder substance of you. It had to be one of the pieces that I had separated. There was no way to hold onto you with my hands.

I learned at my motorcycle instructional course, to turn a tight circle in a small area, required a great amount of skill and concentration. It also necessitated both hands to remain on the handlebars. James, I wondered how exactly I was going to pull that off. I had thought of a way it could be done, but I must admit, I hesitated.

It amazes me what grief can do to a person. A rational person is defined as sensible. They are able to make a decision based upon intelligent thinking. There was absolutely nothing intelligent about what I just did. It was quite impulsive and not very well thought out. Dignity is not an essential requirement for the grief process. The mind only sees what needs to be done and carries it out.

James, if anyone ever knew I did this, they would have thought one of two things.

That I was a completely disgusting human being; or I had completely lost my mind.

I guess I qualified as both. I knew what had to be done so I just did it. I decided to use my teeth to secure you. I pulled my tongue to the back of my mouth so it would not contact you. I had implemented the plan. My heart began to race as I firmly placed my hands on the bars and began to encircle the parking lot. There you were, wedged between my upper and lower front teeth. I guess I did not think it out well enough because you did contact my lips! To do this without the use of my hands, I had to encase my lips around you to release and propel you onto the concrete below.

Oh James, it was such an uneasy encounter. I was confident the camera could never tell the story of what just took place. It could have been interpreted as a piece of chewing gum I suppose. I exited onto the main road and immediately wiped my lips on my shirt. I guess I had to taste you after all.

I was feeling ashamed of myself. How had I allowed myself to do such a thing? I had heard many stories of grief. It drives people to do unspeakable things, but this was by far the worst.

I continued driving down Warwick Avenue. I had almost reached the Cranston line. It was the city that bordered Warwick. It was the place I left so long ago to escape all the rejection. I learned later in life you do not really escape it. It follows you. I left, only to find myself here once again, facing the pain that drove me away.

My eyes caught sight of the bridge. My bike turned left into the parking lot without much thought. I was lucky. It was getting late, and the road was less congested now.

Oh, the memories. The pain. How will I survive this night? Who even knew it would take death, fueled by anger and rejection to allow me to realize the weight of the baggage I had been carrying all these years?

I parked the bike, turned off the engine, and dismounted my shiny white time machine. That was what it felt like now. I wanted to get back to the present, but there was only one way. I had to keep moving forward which required traveling through the tunnel of the past. I stood there trapped between two memories. I could not explain what I was feeling. Something had begun to settle over the stony part of my heart. I was angry at one memory and broken by the other. I had to resolve the one that broke me before I could deal with the one that angered me, or I would have to go back in time. As I said, forward was the only way out. One preceded the other.

I was now aware there was an unfamiliar feeling in the mix that I had not experienced before. I think it was sorrow.

Dear James,

I am standing against the concrete column. It is the only thing separating myself from the small Pawtuxet River below. Before writing to you, I placed my journal on the ledge and stood for just a moment. I remembered I had once researched this place for a history presentation in high school, the year before Adriane was born.

This river played an important role in the early development of the textile industry in New England during the 19th century. It is formed by the confluence of North and South branches of the river at River Point Village in West Warwick. From there, the river continues roughly east through the cities of West Warwick, Warwick, and Cranston, emptying into the Providence River and Pawtuxet Village. The last three miles of the river form the boundary between Cranston and Warwick. It is amazing how much Encyclopedia Britannica had prepared me for all these years later. This is exactly where I am standing James.

I cradled the journal, as I long ago cradled his child, which was now a manuscript filled with a charted course of memories I had been systematically recording.

James,

I just remembered a piece of important information I had written for my presentation so long ago. How ironic! I did not realize it then, but my research forced its way into the scene that took place so long ago. In the native language, the word "Pawtuxet" means "Little falls."

James, there was a fall from this bridge many years ago. You did not witness it; I was the only one who did. I guess I should confess now. At the time, I carried on and pretended I had no knowledge of it. But I honestly never felt guilty. While I am here, we should discuss it.

At that time in our lives, you were working at a local department store. It was 1984 and it was close to Christmas. Adriane was three months old. You had told me you were going out to the gym. Your friend came to pick you up. I do not remember his name, but I do remember his character. It was something you lacked. It is called honesty, James.

You were a thin young man and was always attempting to bulk up, so it did not cause me to be suspicious when you told me you were going to the gym. You left the house and told me you would not be too late. However, what you did not know, nor did I share the information with you, was your friend returned to the house before you did. Remember the character I just told you about?

He told me you did not really go to the gym but went to the Zayre Department Store Christmas party with one of your coworkers you had secretly been involved with. You worked the evening shift as a security guard. Inside your packed bag was the clothing you had planned to wear.

Later that evening, I heard car tires rolling over the crushed stone that filled the driveway. We lived in an apartment that was above a local oil company. They had trucks parked there, and at times when they needed to complete a service call, they would pick one up. I assumed it was one of the vans. I did not realize it was you until your friend had told me he dropped you back off so you could pick up your own car.

He did tell me where I could find you but did not want to get involved. You have to love those people who want to get involved but do not want to get involved. The way I look at it, if you get waist deep in a lake, you might as well jump completely in. You are already wet.

Your niece had spent the night and having been told where you were, I decided to walk there. It was only about a half of a mile from our apartment. Adriane was sleeping comfortably and was not due for a feeding for at least three hours. James, why did you bring her so close to me?

He was right James. You were there. I found your car without any difficulty. It was quite easy to spot. It was a bright orange Dodge Charger which had the Dukes of Hazzard General Lee's Dixie Horn. I was still pregnant when you installed it. The door was unlocked. Without ever seeing a girl, to validate what had been told to me, there on the passenger seat floor was all the proof I needed. You could not miss them. They were a beautiful pair of shiny candy-apple red high heel shoes! I must admit while I am confessing, I was so jealous! I did not own any high heel shoes. I wore jeans or sweatpants and often wore shirts that were yours. These shoes sure were pretty. I thought about going into the bar to confront you, but honestly, I was afraid and embarrassed. I looked down at myself and realized I did not compare to the looks of any girl who owned such nice shoes.

I guess what I did could be defined as childish, but at that moment it was the only thing I could think to do. I removed the shoes and in a fit of rage, I threw them over the bridge into the Pawtuxet River. I watched them splash into water that I am now standing above. They fell fast. I felt a small bit of satisfaction knowing she no longer had any shiny red shoes either. I ran back home praying you did not decide to leave the bar and drive by me.

James did either of you ever wonder what happened to the shoes? You never mentioned it. But then again, why would you?

I realized I had left the little urn in the pouch on my bike. I walked back to collect what I needed, already knowing what I was going to do. I dumped another portion of the ashes into my hand and returned to the bridge. I did not walk as fast as I did the night I threw the shoes. There was no one to be afraid of now. There was no fear of being caught. There was not anyone here tonight that I had to be compared to. There was just an occasional car that drove by, and they were not interested in what I was doing. No one could see what I held. Only I knew the contents of my hand.

July 8, 2016
Friday
11:28 p.m.

Dear James,

I stood at the cement wall of the bridge and got lost in my own thoughts as I stared at the water below. The sound was quite calming. It provided the proper background ambiance needed to clear my mind.

I knew it was time James. I bent carefully over the top of the cement wall. I slowly unfolded my hand after I had rotated my wrist. I released you to the water below. It was quite serene. The night is quiet. The air is still. I watched you evolve into what appeared to be a semi translucent white cloud as you separated into dust-like particles, floating slowly, and disappearing above the water below. It was quite beautiful. You did not try to stop the fall. You made no objection. You willfully descended as if covering the painful memory with yourself.

I did not feel a sense of satisfaction after throwing you over the bridge as I did from the first fall I had witnessed. This fall was much different. It was not a quick decent. There was no audible splash. They were not shoes. It was you.

My heart hurts James. I am feeling quite sad. I feel you slowly leaving completely. Slowly saying goodbye forever.

I quickly went from one memory to another. I had been standing right in the middle of the two of them. The other caught me in its whirlwind the moment I shifted my body's position. It is amazing how two completely different emotions can overlap and blend before the previous completes its own place in time.

It crashed down upon me as an avalanche falling without warning. This one filled my heart with rage. Being lied to always did that to me. Why are emotions so tightly tangled together? Could they ever be sorted out? I tumbled from sorrow to rage instantly.

I had taken Adriane and my niece to get ice cream. She was about three and a half years old. We had not seen James in about a year. We had not seen him since he had gotten married and had another daughter. The day he married, everyone was nervous that I would show up and make a scene. I remember that day. I did not want to be alone. I would be okay if someone were with me. I just could not think of her being surrounded by celebration while I was all by myself at home. I knew I did not want to be his wife. I made that decision about six months prior to the day he married.

A friend stayed with me. We spent part of the day sipping on Seagram's 7 and 7 Up, singing along with songs on MTV, making congratulatory toasts to James and his wife.

After getting both the girls ice cream cones, I continued driving to my apartment. I had picked up my niece from my sister's house in Warwick. She wanted to spend the day with me and Adriane. I had to travel through this familiar place to get to where I lived.

I passed James and his wife on the road. I noticed him immediately. He pulled into the liquor store parking lot immediately after the bridge. It was the same place I found his car the night I had thrown the shiny red shoes to their watery death. There was a bar in the back of the liquor store parking lot. It can be frightening how rejection can make you explode.

I turned my car around and pulled along the right side of his vehicle just as he was exiting the car. His wife remained in the passenger seat.

I told Adriane and my niece, who was a year older, to stay in the car. I approached James without fear. Words were exchanged between us, and his wife got out of the car.

I told her to get back in the car and mind her own business because it had nothing to do with her. She did not listen and came up beside James. He grabbed ahold of my hair, so I immediately grabbed hers.

She was screaming for him to make me let her go. He knew he would not win this way. Hair pulling never hurt me. It infuriated me. So there we were, the three of us all twisted together like a pretzel dropped in a parking lot. He told me he would let go of me if I let go of her. He was not dictating how this was going to happen.

"No!" I told him. "You let go of me then I will let go of her."

Knowing he would not win—or the obvious, he was worried about her—he agreed and let me go. I kept my end of the bargain and let her go. He did not. He picked me up and threw me on top of the hood of my car, causing my head to hit the windshield. I could hear my daughter crying.

When I opened the car door, Adriane climbed out, dropping her ice cream on the ground. He saw her drop it. Only now did I understand this was not in her best interest. I attempted to calm her down, letting him walk away into the store with his wife.

July 8, 2016
Friday
11:58 p.m.

Dear James,

You saw the ice cream fall. I will admit it was my fault. I confronted you. I never blamed you for any of that altercation, but I did hate you for the lack of empathy you showed Adriane. Tonight, I did the same to you. Tonight, it was my choice what would be dropped into the parking lot. It was not ice cream this time. I showed you no sympathy either. I sat down on the ground where she had dropped her ice cream.

James, in case you never watched ice cream on hot cement, it melts. If you do not pick it up immediately, you cannot pick it up. It liquefies.

I made sure you could not be picked up either. I took the water bottle out of the leather saddle bag on the left side of my bike. I put a small handful of you onto the ground. There was no altercation this time, nor was there a struggle. I took the water and poured it on top of you.

The same way I watched Adriane's ice cream become a part of the concrete, I watched you mix with the water until you too could not be picked up. James, just like you did when Adriane dropped the ice cream onto the cement, I stood up and walked away.

I returned to my bike. I knew it was too late to be out on a motorcycle. You increase your chances of being hit by a driver under the influence the later it became.

I attempted to put my right leg over the bike and instantly found myself unable to catch my breath. I hit my knee on the rack behind the seat. I saw stars. I had seen stars once before. I knew this feeling well.

I could not lift myself from the stooped position I immediately found myself in. The pain immobilized me. I dropped the little black urn I had in my hands. I did not try to protect it like I had Adriane. I waited until the pain subsided. I looked for the little urn, picked it up and placed it back in the leather case and took out my journal.

Dear James,

Remember that night? It was our very last time together. You had been living back at your parent's house. You could not make up your mind and honestly neither could I. Thank you for helping me figure it out.

You were going back and forth between me and the girl I had met the day you pushed me down the stairs. Crazy I know. Our toxic relationship occasionally continued even after that. I cannot believe I let you in every now and then when you showed up at my door.

Shamefully, I had become the person you thought I should have been. Maybe this made you want me. I must admit it, alcohol was like drinking liquid courage. Why did I play such a dangerous cat and mouse game with you?

When I was of sober mind, I knew I did not want to be with you. However, when I drank, I was reminded of how empty and lonely my life was. Alcohol made me realize how much I needed to be loved. You had her and I was alone.

I sadly believed alcohol helped me escape the deep void I was so afraid to look at. I cannot believe I convinced myself I would be loved by you if I became what you thought was worthy of love. Remember that, James?

I had been drinking the night before and wanted you to come over. I called you and asked you to come and stay with me and you did. Remember that?

I woke up in the morning feeling frightened and filled with anxiety, regretting once again what I had done. I did not want to be with you, but I did not want to be alone.

I could not take any more lies or the uncertain look you had when you drank. I never knew when you would explode. When you did, I usually ended up underneath a pillow you were forcing down upon my face. I did not want to be afraid anymore. I had watched my mother deal with this, and I wanted a different life for Adriane. Sadly, I was having a hard time learning how to obtain it. I could not find the strength to be alone, but I knew I had to find a way out to protect Adriane.

You woke me up in the morning just before you went to work. We planned to have dinner and talk. James, I had anxiety all day. I was filled with fear. How was I going to tell you I did not really want this? That I did not love you?

I will never forget what I felt when I heard your car pull up. I did not fix supper because I could not do this anymore. Why did I have to call you the night before? I had to tell you the truth. Regardless of how alone I would have to be, I had to do this for her. My life was spiraling out of control.

Do you remember when you walked through the door? You already knew by the way I greeted you. I was holding Adriane. I saw the look on your face, but I had to tell you. You spoke first. I can still hear your words if I close my eyes and recall the memory.

"Look me in the eyes and tell me you do not love me," you screamed. I did not expect your reaction because you had not been drinking.

"I am sorry, James. There is nothing I see in you that I love."

James, I always thought the expression "I saw stars" was nothing more than fabrication to make a story more interesting. It was not. It was the truth. You had hit me many times before, but I always managed to escape before anything serious happened, I felt your fist impact the left side of my head. I saw white floaters which looked like stars. Only two things went through my mind the moment I realized I was falling. One, I was going to die, and the other, I had Adriane in my arms. To protect her, I shifted my position, so she did not become wedged between me and the wall. I held her as tight as I could without hurting her, but tight enough that she did not hit the floor. Everything went black.

Six months later, your girlfriend was pregnant, and you were married.

Hitting my knee on my bike reminded me of that day. I saw the same little floaters, but I did not hit the ground this time. You did, and I did not have Adriane in my arms. I had you.

Tears began to run down my face. Here it was. It had finally arrived. The bottled-up pain finally made its way over the dam I had erected around my heart. The pain I had sworn would never make it out could not be stopped. The force behind it was too powerful.

With tear-filled eyes, I stood up as I did that day and vowed to finish this tonight as I finished it then. This time, I did not feel alone. I knew healing was the only remedy to all this pain. I was surprisingly calm.

This journey was almost done. I gently placed him back into the little black bag on the windshield and pulled out of the parking lot. The ride toward home was quiet. My thoughts were peaceful. The pain in my knee had subsided. I felt the gentle warm wind envelop my whole being as if God were using it to tell me how loved I was, how incredibly proud He was of me and I would *never* be alone. He was there through it all in every detail, then and now. We would finish this together. He was beside me. He always was. I understood that now. I only wish I had then.

As I cautiously rode toward home, I turned the corner onto Broad Street. I found my bike seeming to turn left somehow automatically into a parking lot as if it were being controlled by some other force. There it was! A place I never wanted to see again. Another memory that needed to be dealt with but not one that I wanted to look at. This one was my fault. I still blame myself. I could have stopped it! Why did I not run?

July 9, 2016
Saturday
12:30 a.m.

Dear James,

You did not come to this place with me. I did not come here alone, but I was left to deal with it alone. Later in the evening I had met you back on "The Boulevard." I was supposed to have been resting but I needed someone to acknowledge the emotional turmoil I was in. I could handle the physical part. Pain was something I had been used to. My mother's husband became quite physical after he had enough to drink. Remember how I told you I did not like the effect it had on people? This was why. Little did I know, it would have the same impact on you.

This night, I was certain you would have held me until it all disappeared somehow. I guess I may need to remind you of it. The parking lot is empty now, but on that day it was not.

I had met James in 1982. I was quite innocent when it came to the subject of female reproduction and did not know what the truth was. So many of my friends told me you could not get pregnant the first year after your period began because your body had not yet regulated itself. I was a late bloomer and was not graced with this newfound womanhood until a few months after I turned sixteen. I concluded they had lied or were just too uneducated to know the truth.

James and I were parked in his car, tangled in the back seat. He was so proud of this car. Someone had also told me if you injected Coca-Cola into your vagina, it had the medicinal properties to eradicate sperm. We did not have any of that in the car. There was only a twin-sized yellow-flowered sheet he had brought along for the occasion.

I was not sure how I would get it inside there anyway. After he had ejaculated, I quickly wiped myself off and pulled up my jeans.

As I had said, my mother's husband was an abusive alcoholic. There was no talking anything out. So I tried to ignore the symptoms until I could hide them no longer.

> Yes James, Adriane was our first-born
> child, but one preceded her. Let's talk
> about this. You would not then, but
> tonight you do not have the choice.

I set the little urn on the center of the handlebars against the windshield in case by some chance I could force him to see the building that I did not want to look at.

Prior to the conception of Adriane, I had gotten pregnant at seventeen. My mother's husband made

JOY LATORRE, M.S., APRN-CNP

it a point that my child was to be disposed of. He was the "king of the household," as he called himself, and "the king had spoken."

After much morning sickness and a forced confirmed pregnancy test, my mother contacted a local clinic.

"Just as I predicted," he barked at my mother. "Another one of your slut daughters went out and spread her legs." I suppose there was truth to his accusation. My sister had her first child at sixteen.

He then turned his wrath in my direction. "You will never amount to anything. You are a scumbag just like the rest of your sisters. Get out of my face! You disgust me," he slurred. He was drunk again. What was new?

The appointment had been made. There would be no canceling or rescheduling. It had been chiseled in stone, far too deep for any eraser.

The next morning, my mother brought me to the appointment. There were people walking along the boundary of the property holding signs which we were instructed not to look at. We were told the night before by the staff not to go near them. They kept asking me if I would just talk with them for a moment. A woman who worked in the facility exited the building and escorted me and my mother inside.

After my mother signed some papers giving consent for the procedure, she was given a time to pick me up and she returned home.

I was placed across a desk from a woman who asked me if anyone was forcing me to do this as she continued to push a pen across the paper without ever looking up at me. I looked at her with empty eyes and said no. I did not see any genuine concern in her expression. She was simply carrying out her daily duties at a local abortion clinic that gave her a paycheck at the end of the week. If I had seen an ounce of concern or believed she genuinely wanted to help me protect the child I was so desperately wanting someone to help me save, I might have attempted to escape.

After she signed her name on the paper, I was escorted to the procedure room. I could have been put to sleep for an additional fee, but that would have been asking too much. I had already cost my mother and her husband $175, and trust me, I heard about how he sacrificed to get me out of "the mess I had gotten myself into" every time he had a few drinks for some time after.

I interrupted the memory to pick up the little jar.

"Look James," I screamed. This is where it happened! This time you will listen to what happened inside this building. I was forced to do this alone then, but tonight, you will hear what happened.

I wanted to tell you the night I met you, after the procedure had taken place, but you never asked. You did not ask how I felt. You said nothing! I walked beside you slowly with my hands on my stomach. I wanted you to feel as bad as I did, but you did not speak about it. So, there I was James, lying on an examination table as the doctor entered the room. He explained the procedure while fumbling with some instruments. He explained to me that each instrument was larger in diameter and would progressively dilate my cervix, allowing the entrance of his instrument, which sounded like a vacuum, into my uterus to expel the "products of conception" as he referred to it.

James at seventeen do you think I understood what this meant? I assumed he meant whatever what was growing inside of me. Why didn't he just say baby? That is what it was.

"Is it already formed?" I asked as he was looking at my baby on a screen that was shielded from me. In silence he continued to roll a little ultrasound across my already growing thirteen-and-a-half-week pregnant abdomen.

As if irritated by my question, he turned to the nurse and said it was time to start the procedure. She had given me a Valium prior to the procedure to help me relax which had horribly failed. James, the pain was intense.

"Keep your bottom on the table!" he said sternly. "If you do not stay still, I cannot guarantee that I will get it all out."

Get "it" out James! His words horrified me! What exactly was "it" to him? I knew what "it" was to me.

The cramping was horrendous! It was as if someone had secured a rope around my insides and began pulling them out. It reminded me of a dog tugging on a toy, shaking his head aggressively back and forth attempting to rip it from its master's hand.

James, I tried desperately to distract myself. I began to look around the room. I looked for something to focus on. Something! Anything! My eyes caught sight of a glass jar covered with brown paper. I wondered what it was for. I quickly figured out what it was. It was there to shield its viewer from the contents that made its way down the long plastic tube whose journey began in the hand of the physician. I quickly turned my head when I saw the first spurts of blood splatter onto the inside of the glass container.

However, unlike the master that lets go of the toy in order not to break the dog's teeth, in my case, it did not matter what was broken, they were removing the life completely.

James at that point I became completely void of feeling. I had learned to master that switch in my life. I knew exactly when to turn it on and when to quickly shut it off. Psychologists have coined it survival; I called it insanity. Whichever it was, it temporarily helped me to cope. Feeling as dead inside as our child now was, I surrendered, fully understanding I had been defeated. I let my mind take me to a safer place. A place other than the room I had become hostage to.

After the procedure was over, my legs were released from the stirrups they had been strapped to. I was left alone to get dressed. The nurse returned and placed a large bulky sanitary pad between my legs and walked me through a door to another room. I was placed in a recliner chair and given a blanket as I held onto my now hollow womb. They removed the baby James. The baby was gone.

Truthfully, by the way the nurses lacked eye contact, I wondered who felt emptier, them or their patients. There were many girls in the room. Some crying and others sleeping…and then there was me, emotionless.

As I looked around the room at the faces of all the young girls, I saw one common denominator that no one explained to us when we walked through that door. It was called regret. We were left to deal with that by ourselves. I was left to deal with this alone and once again you were not there.

James, I was able to leave after an hour. The nurse kept checking my sanitary pad to make sure I was not bleeding excessively. I could not wait to leave this place. My mother returned, signed another paper, took me home and never said a word.

I was able to go home, but tonight, you have to stay.

Before starting the engine of my motorcycle, I dropped some of James onto the pavement near the fence. I picked up the journal and finished writing before leaving this place forever.

Dear James,

I left you here for a reason. Promise me one thing? When the sun comes up can you please listen to what the people holding the signs were trying to tell me? It must have been important, because it has always haunted me. It's the least you can do. I hope it's not worse than what I had to endure.

Placing the journal and the little urn back into the pouch, I left the parking lot and headed toward home.

July 9, 2016
Saturday
1:03 a.m.

I drove my motorcycle up the driveway and into the garage. I had left the door open so I could just pull in when I returned. The engine was hot. I could hear the heat clinking off the pipes like the sound of popcorn forced to expand under the right amount of heat. I knew my husband would be worried. It was after midnight now.

He came outside and watched me. "Are you sure you need to do this now?" he asked.

"I know I do," I replied.

"I'll go with you," he responded.

"You go back to sleep, I'll be fine," I answered. After twenty-five years of marriage, he understood me completely. He knew once I started something, I would not stop until it was finished.

Never understanding the concept of a God who loved me so long ago, I thought I was alone. I understood now, I was not alone. I never had been. He was always there.

July 9, 2016
Saturday
1:10 a.m.

Dear James,

I picked up the keys to my car, removed you from the front pocket of my bike and placed you on the front passenger seat of my car. I looked to see how much of you was still in the jar. It was about half full.

It was so quiet in the car. I looked at you as if you could hear and understand me. "James, I do not know where I am going to take you." I said aloud. I thought of turning the car around and having my husband go with me as he suggested. I thought maybe he needed to empty the last pieces of you, but I know in my heart this is between you and me. It started with us and it has to end with us.

I began to drive to a house down off Manton Avenue in Providence, where I had found you when Adriane was about a year and a half old. Well, I did not actually find you. A friend of mine who was dating your brother took me there. It was not for my benefit. I have learned in life most people who tell you something you did not know only tell you when there is something they want to know for themselves. She needed to know if your brother was there. Who better to push in the front door to find out, than the one who was the least afraid? In this friendship, it was me. Do you remember that night James? I will never forget it.

I was going to announce myself the conventional way and knock on the door, but she had a better idea. She told me there was a window in the back of the house. *She obviously had been here before,* I thought to myself but did not speak it out loud.

She hoisted me in through the window. I needed to know if James was in there. I walked through a kitchen and into a dining room. There was a bedroom to the right, and I looked in. There was a nightlight in the room, allowing me to see the two children sleeping side by side. They did not wake at my presence.

I could have been shot for home invasion, but again, none of that mattered now.

There were all types of empty cans and bottles on the table. Everyone was passed out. *How did they not hear me?* There were two girls on the couch sleeping. One girl's feet were lying on the shoulders of the other. They did not move.

There was another room to my right. I entered it and tried to put on the light. It was a pull-string light hanging from the ceiling. It was the room where my friend told me she thought James's brother would be. There was someone in the bed, but it was dark and I could not see.

I got as close as I could, but I could not tell if it was James or his brother. I walked back through the house back to the window where my friend was waiting.

"Was he in there?" she asked.

"I don't know if it is him. Give me a lighter," I demanded.

She quickly took one out of her pocketbook and held it up. I snatched it from her hand, walking back through the rooms in the house. Returning to the one without a light, I stood on the side of the bed and flicked the lighter, illuminating the room. Their heads were covered.

I pulled hard on the blanket. There before me, lying completely nude, were two people.

The girl in the bed reached to the side table and turned on a light. *Ah, there is the light!* I thought to myself.

My friend had nothing to worry about. It was not James's brother before my eyes completely nude with a girl beside him. It was James. *Did he forget he had promised this would never happen again after finding out about "Red Shoes?" That is what I named her in my mind.*

I saw him. What I was dreading paralyzed me. My sympathetic response to fight outweighed the flight, and I sprang into action.

Rage was the only emotion I was capable of at that moment. I screamed at him to get out of the bed. He was startled at first, and then realized he was not dreaming. He attempted to pull the covers over them both. *How dare he! She deserved to be exposed. They both did!* I could smell stale alcohol which saturated the room. He must have told her about me. She did not seem to be surprised at my visitation. She seemed annoyed.

Without reacting in anger, he calmly told me to leave. Leave? *What was he thinking, I was just going to say okay? I will see you when you come home?* When I responded that I was not leaving until he came home, the real James surfaced! He jumped up from the bed and attempted to put sweatpants on, catching his leg on the waistband falling to the floor. I suppose this infuriated him as he became enraged. A crash was the next thing my friend heard. He pushed me into a curio cabinet, knocking the contents off the shelves and shattering the glass. Vulgar language poured from his mouth.

I continued to scream back at him, telling him I was not leaving until he came home with me. He told me to lower my voice because her kids were sleeping.

Her kids?! What about our daughter? my mind roared. *Did he think of her before he got into bed with this woman?* I have never been this bold. I knew better. Anger was something that happened often when he drank.

I never had the chance to tell him the effect this had on me. More humiliating than having him insult or hit me in front of this girl was what I did when we got home.

He had to drive me because my friend left when she heard the commotion. I guess she got the answer she was looking for. His brother was not there.

Dear James,

This is almost too embarrassing to write but how will anyone understand how desperate I was to be loved? It is a part of this journey. Truth must be told for healing to happen. I brought Adriane to my sister's house before I set off to help my friend, so we were alone.

When we arrived at home, you went into the house first. You attempted to escape the situation and go to bed. Do you remember me stopping you? Do you remember what I said to you, James? It still haunts me to this very day. I did not ask. I begged.

A counselor once explained to me the difference between two words. She said they were often confused with one another—*shame* and *embarrassment*. *Embarrassment* is what a person feels after they have done something which causes them to feel shame. *Shame*, however, is embarrassment of who you are. The following account is my personal definition of shame, and I understand I must expose it to be free of it.

Once we were both back inside the house, I began to remove my clothing in front of him.

"Look at me!" I screamed. "What is wrong with me?"

He continued to sit there, his head buried in his hands.

"Look at me!" I screamed again. "Why am I not good enough? Why am I not sexy enough for you?" As he continued to sit motionless, I became more desperate.

He got up to walk away into the bedroom, and I gently pushed him back onto the couch.

"Please," I begged him, crying. "Please love me." Sadly, I had believed sex was love. *If this was love, why did I feel so completely empty?*

Once again, he hung his head into his hands. *What did he think? Did he think I was disgusting? Did he loathe me?* Regardless of what I had to do, I knew I had to get him to have sex with me.

In our relationship, there were sexual things he would ask me to say to arouse him. I never would. However, I knew tonight I had to do whatever he asked of me to get him to have sex with me. *He finally won*, I thought.

I knew this was not making love. It had nothing to do with love. It was perversion. It was disgusting to even say, but I said what I knew he wanted to hear. The very sound of my own voice repulsed me.

Never did I think it would leave me emptier than I already was. After he ejaculated, he left me lying on the floor where we were. He went to bed and fell asleep.

Dear James,

You never knew what I did after that.

You had no trouble falling back to sleep.

I sobbed, listening to you snore. How could my life be any more broken than it already was at that moment? Never had I felt so abandoned. So unloved. So dirty.

I could not shower. The tub was filled with Adriane's clothes that had been soaking. Our tub had also been my washing machine. The sink would have to do. After wiping as much of what just happened off of me, I got into the bed beside you. I could not sleep against you. All I could smell was the perfume of another woman. I had to get as far away from you as I could. I crawled as close to the edge of the other side of the bed. Without making any noise, I cried myself to sleep.

When I opened my eyes in the morning, I fully understood how broken and ashamed I was. In my desperate need for stability, even if it was insane, I got up before you woke and made you breakfast. Sadly, I believed that to be loved, I had to earn love. I learned this from my mother.

I decided not to take James back to that awful house. He never belonged there. He belonged with me and Adriane. It broke my heart to find him there. Not even anger could get me to bring him there. Even he did not deserve that.

I intuitively knew we had to visit two more places. These last places were not to cover the feelings I had for myself but for a daughter that was born out of what we had. Good or bad, it gave me my daughter.

I turned the car around and started driving toward the hospital where Adriane was born. When I arrived, I parked the car and looked at the building. The parking lot was dark and just about empty. I tried to remember what door we went through. James, his mother, and I were greeted by a receptionist.

"Good evening. May I help you?" she asked me.

"I think I am in labor," I answered, trying to catch my breath in between the vise-like pain that was again squeezing my abdomen. James and his mother did not come with me to the glass window that surrounded the woman taking my information.

"Okay," she stated. "What is your name and when is your due date?" I told her my name and that I was due on September 2. *The date was now Friday, September 14, 1984.* She had me take a seat while she walked into the back where I could no longer see her.

We only waited a short time before I was taken to be examined. I was not upset that James did not come with me. His mother was with us. I did not want her to join us and see me naked. After I was examined, my labor was confirmed. She told me to walk the halls. Without the display of any sympathy for my pain, she advised me I was only in early labor and it would be many hours before I delivered. I returned to the waiting room and sat with James and his mother. She did have me change into a hospital gown prior to examining me which I was still wearing. I remember how cold the furniture was on my skin.

The nurse had made me feel so unimportant. I was now wishing James had gone in the back with me. Once again, the cramping in my stomach began. I tried to sit quietly. James got up to go to the bathroom. Did it make him nervous? I honestly did not know because he didn't say anything.

By the time he returned from the bathroom, the pain had subsided. He told me he was going to take his mother home and come back. I did not want to be alone but agreed. It would not take that long. The hospital was not that far from his parent's house. I walked here often for my prenatal appointments. He would have plenty of time before we had our baby. According to the nurse, I had until the morning. It was only ten thirty. They left and I sat in the quiet with my thoughts.

Dear James,

Can I tell you what happened after you left? I tried walking for a little while. I did everything the nurse had asked me to do. I was always trying to please other people so they would like me and be kind. However, I did not last long. I thought I would at least make it until you got back. I tried to wait for you. I really did. Trust me, I did not want to go back there alone again, but I could not take the pain any longer. I was hesitant to return to the nurse who told me to go and walk. She was reading the newspaper and drinking coffee when I returned. She did not hear me as I had these little rubber foam slippers on my feet which she gave me. I apologized for bothering her. How timid I was then. She just grumbled quietly, but loud enough for me to hear. "Babies having babies," she said. I felt so ashamed.

James, she could have made Adriane's birth so much less frightening if she had been kind to me. I did everything I could to try and make her like me. What I did not understand then, but understand now, was she did not like herself. I was just the person she blamed it on.

"Get up on the stretcher," she said without looking at me. "First babies take a long time. You are not
going to have this baby for at least another twelve
hours, if not longer," she grumbled. She placed a
cold silver disk on the top of my stomach that was
secured by a Velcro strap.

"Can I ask a question?" I said after taking ten
minutes to muster up the guts.

"What is it?" she snapped without emotion.

"When my boyfriend gets back, will he be able
to come back in?" She did not answer me immediately. She was fussing with a roll of paper that she
was trying to get into some sort of a machine. I did
not dare ask what it was. Once she had it securely in
its place, her question shocked me.

"Is he the father?" she asked.

"Yes," I answered. *How humiliated she was making me feel. I already felt so all alone. Of course, he is
the father!* I screamed silently to myself.

> James, why did you have to leave? I
> began to experience such bad pain.
> I only needed to know I was not
> alone. This nurse was making me
> feel so unwanted. I began to cry for
> so many reasons. I was filled with
> fear. I did not even want to think of

the pain it would cause to have this little human exit my body.

The thought that was more paralyzing, was that I was going to die, and I was alone.

I must have been upsetting the nurse. It was evident she was irritated. After all, she had to deal with a crying 18-year-old. She made that quite clear.

I tried so hard to remain as calm as I could. I tried to be a good patient. She was the only person with me. I needed her to want to comfort me.

The pain returned, causing me to lose control. I remember saying, that I could not do this any longer more than once. She figured a way to make me be quiet I suppose, although I objected to her plan. James, I saw the needle. It was only then that I did not feel so timid.

"What are you going to do?" I asked.
"You need to calm down. I told you, first babies take a long time. You need to sleep," she barked.

"I don't want a needle. I will be quiet. I promise," I tried to say in a convincing voice. "Please, I don't want a needle," I repeated.

She rolled me onto my side and sunk what looked like a harpoon into my left-top buttock.

"Now settle down," she said. "You are in for a long night."

Dear James,

I remember looking at the clock. It was 11:30 p.m. You should have been back by now. Where were you? I remember whatever was in that needle made me feel very dizzy. The room began to violently spin. I thought if I closed my eyes, it would stop. It did help the pain I suppose because I fell asleep.

It was not long before my eyes sprang open. For just a moment I did not understand where I was. The unbearable pain instantly reminded me. My mother was now seated beside me. I asked her if you were here. Without warning, it happened. I began to vomit.

All I remember was every time the pain came, my stomach felt like a rock and I heaved. James, I never knew puke could come out of your nose. I just wanted to go home. I knew it was not an option, but my thoughts were irrational. I had to somehow escape everything that was happening.

I was suddenly aware of a horrific burning sensation between my legs and I started screaming that my crotch was on fire. I kept putting my hands there. I do not know why. Maybe it was just a natural reaction. Did I do it because I thought I could make it stop?

"Get your hands out of there!" the nurse yelled when she came back into the room. Did this woman have any emotion other than anger?

She attempted to now convince my mother I was just being hysterical. I guess my last words finally got her attention.

"It's ripping!" I was screaming at the top of my lungs.

The nurse took one look between my legs and crossed them tightly. She instantly looked as frightened as I felt.

"I need to get her into the delivery room now," she told my mother. I only remember the sound of the metal bars on the sides of the stretcher that clicked as she pulled them up before moving me. I looked frantically around the room. Where were you? Why was it taking you so long? The room was still spinning, and I continued to vomit on the way down the hallway to our next destination.

I managed to somehow look at the clock hanging on the wall she crashed the head of the bed into. My body jolted. This felt like something out of a horror movie. The room stopped spinning long enough for me to see it was 12:20 a.m. I did not know where you were, James, but it did not take two hours to travel less than three miles down the road and back.

The nurse began to move me from the stretcher to a silver table that had a large light suspended above my body. I was cold. At that moment I was thankful for the foam slippers she gave me because they shielded my feet from the two metal cold objects on both sides of me that looked like horse stirrups.

When the doctor entered the room, I was amazed at how nice the nurse became. She kindly told me not to push. The baby's head was right there. She told me the doctor needed time to get gloves on and make sure it was safe for the baby to come out.

Safe, I thought to myself. Why would it not be safe?

The doctor was a familiar face. I had seen him during my visits to the clinic to measure my growing stomach and listen to the perfect tempo of this little human's heartbeat. It was something that always put a smile on my face. Although he was anxiously trying to slip into a blue covering the nurse was attempting to tie in the back, his presence made me feel safer.

After putting on rubber gloves that almost met his elbows, he assumed his position between my legs. James, I felt so violated! I felt like a lab specimen that was being examined. Yes, you and I had sex. That is why I was in this situation, but no one had ever put my private parts on display under a light. At least not that I remember. I suppose the abortion clinic I left James at qualified. He positioned the light right between my legs. He looked at me and told me to take some slow deep breaths very gently. His presence calmed me.

I then heard him speak in a loud tone. I was relieved when I realized it was not me he was talking to, but the nurse that kept telling me our baby was not going to be born for at least 12 hours.

"Okay," the doctor said in a gentle voice. "I need you to listen to me. With the next contraction, I need you to take a deep breath, hold it in, and push as hard as you can."

The pain had already started before he finished his sentence, and I did what he told me.

The nurse, who had now become my best friend, was telling me what a good job I was doing. I do not know why her personality abruptly changed, but I welcomed it. The burning between my legs felt like someone was pouring burning oil on me. I burned my fingertips in grease once, and it was the only thing I could slightly relate it to.

"The head is out," he said. "Slow deep breaths. When the contraction begins again, I want you to do just what you did the last time. The shoulders are wider, so I need you to push hard." His calm reassuring voice somehow kept me more focused feeling more in control.

The pain started. I drew in a deep breath. I felt the pressure between my legs once again. I began to push, knowing the burning would return. It did, with a vengeance.

However, after the last push, the burning stopped. I felt what was a weird bumpy, slippery sensation as our baby fully exited my body.

"It's a girl," the nurse said.

"A girl? I have a little girl," I said with tears in my eyes. "We have a girl," I said happily. Only to realize you were not there.

James our daughter was born at 12:41 am. A little over two hours after getting to the hospital, and you were not here. Where were you? That thought did not matter after I realized there was something wrong. The expression on the nurse's face told me a story I did not want to hear.

"Why isn't my baby crying?" I asked softly.

I saw the doctor's eyes turn to the nurse.

"What did you give her?" the doctor demanded.

"Demerol," the nurse answered. "What time?" he jolted back. "About 45 minutes ago."

"Get someone down here now!" he screamed. "You medicated her too close to the birth of this baby!"

James, I was confused. This fear was far greater than the one I was feeling when I felt there was a watermelon trying to exit from an area that now felt quite swollen. I was not understanding what they were talking about. The nurse went to the desk and he remained down between my legs. I still did not hear our baby. Not even a little whimper.

A few other people hurried into the room. The doctor who delivered her remained where he was, and our little girl was handed over to another man who had entered the room. That was the first time I saw her. She did not look normal to me. She was blue.

"Why is my baby not crying?" I asked again. Nobody answered me.

I looked over in the direction of where they were. "Come on, little girl," they kept saying. "Come on, breathe."

"She's not breathing?" I asked.

They were undisturbed by my question as they, too, were preparing a needle. They gave my daughter a shot of something and continued to move her all around, hitting the bottom of her feet.

My mother had made her way to the room where I delivered her. I had noticed her standing in the doorway as my eyes darted around the room looking for someone to answer me.

"Mom," I pleaded. "Why is she not crying?" I saw fear on her face, and my heart filled with panic. I do not know if she answered. After what felt like an eternity, I heard the faintest little cry. It was not until that very moment that all my fear and pain vanished.

"Welcome to the world, little girl," I heard them say.

The moment the memory faded, and I realized I was still sitting in the car. I turned off the engine, got out of the car, locked the door, and walked across the parking lot to the front door. The street was abandoned. I saw not a single person. I was thankful as I did not want anyone to ask me if I needed any help. I approached an automatic door, immediately remembering it as the door we entered the night Adriane was born. I had learned the hospital closed its maternity ward a year after Adriane was born. I always wondered what happened to that nurse.

I was getting tired. Leaving the car seemed to help. The air outside was now cooling. As it touched my face, it seemed to jolt me back from my sleepiness. This place took no thought at all. I knew exactly what I needed to do. I had the urn with me. I looked around for cameras. I did not see any. It did not matter if I did; it had to be done. I knew this could not be a small drop, but the rest of what was left in the jar. *Why would it not be?* I thought to myself. *It is where James left the greatest part of himself. For me, it was where my greatest heartbreak took place. It was not the lying. It was not the cheating. It wasn't even the physical abuse he inflicted upon me. The greatest pain he ever caused, was not being there when Adriane entered the world. She would not remember. But again, my heart told me that night exactly what I had known all along.*

I took the journal out and penned what I was feeling.

July 9, 2016
Saturday
12:41 a.m.

Dear James,

I knew I had to leave the rest of you here. This is where you left us. You know exactly what that means, James. You never came back. I waited. A young girl so hopeful that life would now change for me. I somehow believed my child would never have to face all the rejection I had endured as a young girl. She would never have to listen to someone tell her that her father was not there. Sadly, it had become the reality I dreaded.

They stabilized Adriane and wrapped her little body in a blanket and placed her in my arms. I was captivated by her little face. I remember being slightly hesitant to take her as my body had been shaking although I was not cold. The nurse covered me with a blanket. She assured me it was from the birth. My body had lost seven pounds of added heat. I smiled. I uncovered her little hands to count her fingers. Her skin was peeling at the creases of her wrist. Her little fingernails were paper thin. *So delicate*, I thought.

I must admit, I was not thinking of James in this moment until the nurse decided to ask.

"Is daddy coming back?" she asked.

I did not know what to say because I did not know where he was. However, I found myself immediately making up an excuse for his absence. Was it for him or was I subconsciously trying to alter my current reality?

"He was very tired. He had a long day at work and may have fallen asleep when he took his mom home. Do you have a phone I can use?" I asked.

She handed me a phone, and I called his mother's house. I told her the baby was born, and we had a little girl. She congratulated me but told me James was not there. She did tell me he was going to stop at his sister's house before coming back to the hospital. I thanked her and told her I would call her house.

I hung up the phone and called his sister. She answered. There was so much noise in the background. I was confused. It was almost one thirty in the morning.

Dear James,

Did you forget? Did you forget that I was in labor? Did you forget that your first child was entering the world and you were not here to meet her? I felt like it took forever for you to come to the phone. When you did, my heart felt suffocated. Do you remember the conversation James? I do.

"Hi," I said. "We had a little girl."

(The sound of laughter.)

What are you doing?"

"Playing Monopoly," he answered.

What was he talking about? Was this some kind of a cruel joke? "Why didn't you come back?" I asked him.

"I tried. They wouldn't let me in," he said. "I'll see you tomorrow. They are yelling at me because it is my turn to move. Give her a kiss for me," he said, followed by the sound of a dial tone. Completely shocked by what just happened, I continued an imaginary conversation into a phone James had so quickly disconnected.

"Oh, she is so beautiful!" I said.

(Dial tone.)

"She was born at 12:41 a.m."

(Dial tone.)

"Yes! She was a perfect weight. She is seven pounds, one and a half ounce."

(Dial tone.)

"I completely understand. Get some sleep. We will see you in the morning. Yes, I will give her a big kiss for you."

(Dial tone.)

"Okay. Good night. I love you too."

To cover my embarrassment, I had to try to fool a nurse who already knew the truth. I pressed the receiver to my ear as hard as I could, so she did not hear what I was listening to on the other end of the receiver. I always wondered if she heard the dial tone too. I hate to admit it, but she was right all along, I suppose. Just babies having a baby.

I handed the phone back to the nurse. Her expression said not only what I knew she was thinking but also what my heart was attempting to deny long before I entered that hospital to deliver Adriane. Her piercing gaze spoke loud and clear, point proven. She communicated without speaking a single word as she once again covered my shaking body with her blanket of shame.

It's going to be okay my little love. We have each other, I thought as I brought her closer to my heart.

July 9, 2016
Saturday
1:18 a.m.

Dear James,

I emptied the little jar without worrying who would see me this time. I had to. Without fear or hesitation, I poured you out onto the metal track that held the automatic doors. You always said they would not let you in, but I knew it was not the truth. After Adriane was born, a friend of my mother's arrived. Maybe my mother called her because she thought our daughter was not going to make it.

You were not there that night. You were not visible to anyone. Tonight, you are very much visible. You are all over the entrance of the door. I wondered for a moment if your new form would interrupt the function of the door. I was a little nervous watching as it began to close. Thankfully, you did not.

If anyone checks to see if you came back, they would know that you finally arrived.

James, the reason I dumped you across the threshold of the automatic door was simple.

I desperately needed you to be present the day our daughter was born, and you remained absent.

Adriane was born here, and I was alone. She almost died here, and I was alone. It was the very first night that I realized there was

something wrong with our baby's
eyes, and I was alone. It was the
day she entered this world, and her
father was not there. We were alone.
You were drinking and playing
Monopoly. She took her first breath
while everyone in the room waited
with intense fear. She spent the first
night of her life beside her mother,
without being held by her father.

I stepped away from the automatic door and
watched it close one last time. "Goodbye, James", I
whispered. "I somehow know you understand."

I returned to my car. There was a stadium style
light that illuminated the parking lot, allowing me
to make it back to the car safely. I could not believe
how quiet it was. Just me and my own thoughts.

I opened the car door. Soliloquy entered, taking
her seat beside me. She sat quietly. We both closed
our doors simultaneously. She was me. I was her.

I pulled down the visor and looked in the mirror at the person staring back at me. Soliloquy spoke
softly. "Life has changed you so much. All this pain
has caused you to build a wall around your heart, a
wall that has kept people at a secure enough distance
allowing you the safety you needed. It is time to stop
fighting. It is time to destroy the walls."

I turned to look at my other half sitting beside me. *We are almost done*, I said. Seeing strength enter her fragile existence, I gently smiled. We will do this together. I am so proud of you. Thank you for joining me.

There was a place that Adriane and I had gone together before returning her to Boston to board her plane home. It was not a planned trip. It was spur of the moment. We were doing a few last-minute errands. She was telling me how she felt the night of the wake. I listened to her heart through her words. "I've always felt last, Mom. Even at the wake, I had to be the last one to look at him."

She sat with her face looking out the passenger window. I don't think she was trying to look at anything. She was trying to hide her expression. I pulled into the nearest parking lot to turn the car around. With a determination I wished I had so many years ago, we headed back toward Warwick. There was no army that could have ever stopped the mission I decided to conquer.

Dear James,

I cannot help but think about the first day Adriane and I picked you up. I had to do it James. I hope it did not upset you. I called the funeral home to see if I could get a part of you before anyone else had the chance to. I had to make sure she was first. She felt so insignificant at your wake. So forgotten. I did it for Adriane, but I would be lying if I said I did not want it too. We were just about to head toward Boston, and I turned to her and said, "Not this time Adriane. This time you will be first." I called the funeral home and explained to them who I was. I told them Adriane was your eldest child and she did not live in the United States. I told the man who answered the phone, she had to be back in Boston for a one o 'clock flight. I told him my intention was to purchase an urn from their facility, after he advised me they sold them. I did not want to push my luck and tell him I needed enough of you for the both of us. I was told that they had to contact your brother's wife for permission as they were the couple that arranged the cremation and paid for the services. James, the funeral home knew Adriane was

your child. They printed the obitu-
ary your family provided. He continued to tell me that you would not be
ready. Ready? Were you in the process of being cremated as we spoke?
How long did the process even take?
The thought was haunting.

James, he did call me back.
Your brother gave him permission
to release some of you to us, whatever that would even look like. I
was surprised it was not your wife
who was handling your services but
at the same time I was grateful. I do
not know what her response would
have been.

James, I felt compelled to tell
them a short version of our story.
Moved by empathy for Adriane, he
told us to come at 11:00 a.m. Your
family was picking you up at 1:00
p.m.

When Adriane and I arrived to pick up the ashes,
we looked at the choices of small urns they sold. I
wondered what would go better with the coloring of
my décor. Silly, but true. I knew James liked black,
so we decided on a gold-and-black urn. It would do.

I knew this was my chance to take some of James for myself. I asked the man if I could buy two urns. What salesman would turn down the opportunity of a sale? After all, they were sixty-five dollars each. We waited in the office while he went to get what we came for. *Why was my stomach flipping?* I thought. *Was it because I was nervous about having one of his family members arrive before we had the chance to leave or that they were scooping James into a jar?* He returned offering his condolences and wished Adriane a safe flight home.

Thanking the man and feeling like I vindicated my daughter, we returned to the car with the box containing the two small urns, one for me and one for her.

Dear James,

What a creepy feeling this was. I wanted so badly to remove the top of the jar so I could look inside to see what you looked like, but I was a little scared. I could not believe this is how you ended up. Dust crammed into a little urn. I also wondered how much dust was made from cremating an entire human body. I hoped there was enough for the rest of your family, but I must admit there was a sense of satisfaction and accomplishment when I got Adriane back to the airport. When I took her suitcase out of the trunk and she had to unzipper it to place you in it, my heart broke. You know what she said James? These were her words. "Mom what if they take him away from me? What if they think it is a hand grenade when they scan my luggage? James, I must admit, it made us giggle. I was grateful for the small moment of laughter during this awkward situation.

It broke my heart when she said the next sentence. She tried to make light of a very heavy situation. "This is one way he gets to see where I live." James, I wonder can you see all of this now? Can you see how beautiful she is? I sure hope you can see the Netherlands. It is beautiful where she lives.

I walked Adriane to the gate. She was nervous, and I always worried about her getting lost with her limited vision. I told the woman at the scanner she had cremated remains in the suitcase. She looked at us with understanding. She assured Adriane they would not be confiscated.

Before Adriane walked through the boarding gate to return home, she asked one final question.

"Mom," she hesitated, "what am I supposed to do with him?" I answered without hesitation because I knew it to be true of my own little urn.

"You will know what to do with him when the time is right," I answered. "I love you. That is why I made sure you returned home feeling first. In my heart, you always came first." She smiled. I watched her as she walked through the security gate with the chaperone that guided her to board her flight home.

It was a long ride home from Boston. I never did understand why people honked horns at each other knowing the traffic was the problem. They did it anyway. I suppose it was the only way to express their frustrations. I just ebbed and flowed with the cars. Nothing ever seemed to bother me after dropping her off. I felt that old familiar feeling of loss every time she boarded the plane. I remained quiet throughout the rest of the day. I will feel better tomorrow. I reassured myself.

July 9, 2016
Saturday
1:30 a.m.

As I drove toward our last stop, so many memories poured into my mind. They were not memories of our past nor of my future. They were not my right or his wrong, my pain or his lack of apology. They were lessons God had taught me over the years as Adriane grew, times when my heart was so overwhelmed, lacking understanding.

In those moments, He taught me the greatest lessons, unexpected ones you could not prepare for. Instruction that was easily accepted as it was untainted by human understanding. Lessons that snuck up and showed me truth when God knew my heart was ready.

As I continued to drive toward our destination, in my mind, I was instantly transported back to a time when Adriane was thirteen. It was as if I was standing in a room watching the scene unfold. I was both in the room and looking into it. This is what I saw:

The room was full. Our newest little family member had made his first public appearance at Sunday dinner. I watched my eighteen-year-old nephew Peter attempt to hold his newborn cousin Marc. He was trying to be so careful with him. He captivated me. I watched his movements and facial expressions. He looked at my sister-in-law for reassurance. He did not know whether to cradle him in his arms or attempt to place him in the burping position. I looked intently at his face. His eyes searched for affirmation that he was doing fine at his attempt to comfort the baby as his little cry permeated the room. He decided on the cradle position, but the baby's head fell a little too soon as he tried to lower him into the crook of his arm.

July 9, 2016
Saturday
1:48 a.m.

I pulled into the parking lot of our final destination. It was close to two in the morning. I was tired, but I knew I had to complete this tonight. The pain was right at the brim of my throat.

I parked the car, so it was facing the building. Soliloquy spoke not a word. I understood she no longer needed the protection of my walls. At one time, they served her, but she no longer wanted to stay. I protected her all these years, and now it was her turn to strengthen me. She smiled, touching my arm gently. The car door opened, and she was gone.

I looked at the building located at the edge of the parking lot. This was the place where James signed the adoption papers relinquishing all his rights as Adriane's father.

I reached into my front pocket, scooping up its contents. I held what I still had left of James in my hand. I held his dust.

A book I had once read for a grief group spoke about dust. In her book *It's Not Supposed to Be This Way*, Lysa TerKeurst wrote, "But what about those times when things aren't just broken but shattered beyond repair? Shattered to the point of dust? At least when things are broken, there is some hope you can glue the pieces back together. But what if there are not even pieces to pick up in front of you? You cannot glue dust."[4]

In my mind, I once again saw my nephew trying to cradle his new baby cousin. I watched him with loving eyes. How frightened he was.

At that very moment, I heard the Lord speak gently to my heart, "Look at him."

"I am," I answered.

"Tell me what you see," He asked.

"I see a young man trying to hold a small baby, so unsure of himself."

"That is what you think you see," He said gently.

"I don't understand," I whispered.

"Look deeper," He spoke. "This is what your eyes once saw, but tell me what your heart sees now."

I dropped my head and wept. Finally understanding what He was trying to show me, I answered, "I see James, Lord. My heart sees James."

I turned my face toward heaven, asking some questions of my own. "Is this what you meant by dust when I read that book? Is this what you meant when the writer said you do your best work with dust? Was this always your plan? To cover all this pain with his dust. I cannot glue it, Lord. It is broken beyond repair. It is dust!"

"Open your hand," I heard Him say to my heart.

I looked down at the pieces of James I was still cradling in my hand. I realized one of them looked much more broken and oddly shaped than the two white ones beside it.

"What do I do with them?" I asked.

God spoke tenderly again. "Keep the most broken piece to always remind you of what I always saw. Allow yourself to see James how I saw him and forgive him. He was broken."

I closed my fist tightly around the small dark piece of James I had secured in the palm of my hand and began to cry. I could not stop my body from uncontrollably shaking.

I am sorry, James. I sobbed. I am sorry that I did not see your brokenness. I am sorry that I only saw my own pain. I am so sorry it ended this way.

July 9, 2016
Saturday
2:21 a.m.

The words of Lysa's book flashed before my eyes again. "Dust doesn't have to signify the end. Dust is often what must be present for the new to begin."

This is not the end, I thought. *It is the beginning.*

My mind immediately returned to the dream I had before I learned that James had died. Inside his long black coat, perfectly arranged, were tiny pieces of pussy willows. I was not surprised to learn the bark of a willow contained salicin, a chemical similar to a pain reliever. Something he had gently placed over my heart in a dream, I now understood.

I took the broken little piece of James and placed it into the jar. I opened my hand and released the rest of him into the parking lot to symbolically cover the final memory. I tightly held the little urn and closed the window. Before putting the car into drive, I wrote in the journal for the last time, only after I spoke it aloud.

"Thank you, God," I whispered into the star-filled sky. "Thank you for doing your best work with dust. You found a way to cover all of this pain with his dust."

I smiled as I closed the book gently and placed it on the seat beside me. "Rest in peace, James," I whispered as the last tear slowly descended down my face, landing on top of the little ceramic urn.

Acknowledgments

In life, there are those special people, the few who see your vision and are willing to help you make it reality. I must first thank Molly Pangburn. Thank you for reminding me that this story was not mine but God's. He knew you would nudge me when I needed it. It did not need to be perfect. I only needed to be willing to share it. Mistakes are there to remind us God's love does not require perfection. To Him, we are always perfect. If it were not for your love and friendship, this book would never have gone into print.

To my husband, Paul, your love continues to far surpass any love I have known in human form. You saw something in me no one else took the time to look for. Thank you for seeing it. As broken as I was, your love completed me. God knew it would. It was much easier to arise from the ashes with you by my side. Thank you for loving Adriane and showing her what human fatherly love was supposed to look like.

To Jenny Tufano, you have been a constant in my life from the first day I began to desperately search for a way out of my own despair. Thank you for being there when I finally decided I could not do life alone. You have guided me through so many things in my life. I am eternally grateful for your gentle friendship.

To Jacqueline Strothoff, my first spiritual mother, thank you for the love you and Bob poured into my little family. Thank you for being the person Adriane and I had beside us when she spoke her final words to a man who biologically fathered her. Your love and presence gave us both the strength we needed fourteen years before his death. I will leave that story for her to write.

Rebecca Danielle at Radiance Photography and your beautiful daughter Savannah, thank you. You brought to life what I saw in my heart through the lens of your camera. You are a magnificent young woman, and Savannah is blessed to call you mommy.

Savannah, you were the perfect little girl for this photograph for more than one reason. It is a story I know your mommy will tell you someday.

Marissa Pennington, I could never thank you enough for the patient person you are. You tirelessly changed the cover, colors, font, and design until it became a beautiful work of art! You truly are a gift to this world.

My friend Stacie, thank you for being my sounding board. Your input was invaluable. At times, it felt like you were helping me arrange word tiles I could not arrange alone. The laughs were fun.

Finally, to James, thank you for the life you gave to Adriane. God in heaven knew you and I were the only two people that could have made her exactly the way she is. She is perfect. Again, I forgive you completely. My prayer is that you are now resting peacefully in the arms of the only one who ever completely understood all that you carried inside your heart. Rest in peace.

Notes

[1] Lord A. Tennyson, "In Memoriam A.H.H.," (Edward Moxon, Dover Street, London, 1850).

[2] Adele Adkins & Greg Kurstin, "Hello," from the album *25*, (XL Recordings, Columbia, 2015, Copyright Universal Music Publishing Group, United Kingdom), https://www.umusicpub.com/uk/Artis ts/A/Adele.aspx.

[3] Kelly Clarkson & Greg Kurstin, "Piece by Piece," from the album *Piece by Piece*, (RCA Records, 19 Recordings, Inc., 2014), Remix (RCA Records, March 4, 2016), *American Idol* version.

[4] Lysa TerKeurst, *It's Not Supposed to Be This Way: Finding Unexpected Strength When Disappointments Leave You Shattered* (Nashville: Nelson Books, an imprint of Thomas Nelson, Harper Collins Christian Publishing Inc., 2018), 17–18.

About the Author

Joy LaTorre was born in Providence, Rhode Island. She graduated with a master of science and is a certified family nurse practitioner specializing in end-of-life care. Her studies included courses in thanatology and grief.

She is the founder of Build the Banner of Love Inc., a nonprofit organization supporting families through grief after the loss of a loved one due to a substance-related death.

She is happily married to her husband, Paul, of thirty years. Together, they have three children: Adriane Michelle, Brianna Marie, and Paul Michael. They presently have four granddaughters: Mikaelah Annabelle, Aubrey Katherine, Skylar Rae, and Brooklynn Rose.

They live in Cranston, Rhode Island, with their standard poodle Solomon.

CPSIA information can be obtained
at www.ICGtesting.com
Printed in the USA
BVHW021921100422
633833BV00004B/86